MI5 and Me

MI5 and Me

A Coronet Among the Spooks

Charlotte Bingham

BLOOMSBURY PUBLISHING
LONDON · OXFORD · NEW YORK · NEW DELHI · SYDNEY

BLOOMSBURY PUBLISHING
Bloomsbury Publishing Plc
50 Bedford Square, London, WC1B 3DP, UK

BLOOMSBURY, BLOOMSBURY PUBLISHING and the Diana logo are trademarks of
Bloomsbury Publishing Plc

First published in Great Britain 2018

A catalogue record for this book is available from the British Library

Library of Congress Cataloguing-in-Publication data has been applied for

ISBN: HB: 978-1-4088-8814-8; TPB: 978-1-4088-8815-5; EBOOK: 978-1-4088-8816-2

2 4 6 8 10 9 7 5 3 1

Typeset by Integra Software Services Pvt. Ltd.
Printed and bound in Great Britain by CPI Group (UK) Ltd, Croydon CR0 4YY

To find out more about our authors and books visit www.bloomsbury.com
and sign up for our newsletters

This book is dedicated to Alexandra Pringle who not only encouraged it from the start, but was its guardian angel reading each chapter as I finished it and responding with the kind of words authors treasure. Without her this might never have been written.

'Let other pens dwell on guilt and misery. I quit such odious subjects as soon as I can, impatient to restore everybody not greatly in fault themselves to tolerable comfort, and to have done with all the rest.'

Jane Austen, *Mansfield Park*

The action of this book takes
place in England in the 1950s.

THE FACTS OF LIFE

It seems to me now that everyone who came to our house in those days was a spy.

I had always thought my father did something really boring at the War Office because that was what he told me, and since he went around looking vague and rather bored and wearing clothes that seemed to go with the job, I believed him. No, actually, I didn't believe him; I just wasn't interested in anything he was doing, only what I was doing, or rather – what I was not doing. Then one ghastly rainy day, when I was getting on my mother's nerves even more than usual, he called me into the drawing room.

I didn't realise then that my father frightened everyone, not just me. This particular day his face wore the expression of someone who was about to tell me something I didn't want to know, so I tried to look young and vulnerable, but I saw he was going to tell me anyway.

As I stood there in dreadful silence waiting, a horrid thought came into my mind, a thought more frightening even than my father. He might be going to tell me the Facts of Life, but following that I quickly reassured myself that he *couldn't* be going to tell me because he definitely didn't know them. I mean parents just didn't, did they – they were parents, for heaven's sake. They told you off, and moaned about school fees, and generally found you a pain, but they didn't do It. They couldn't. Apart from anything else, it would mean stubbing out their cigarettes, or putting their drinks down.

The room was still filled with an Awful Silence so I looked about me wondering if he had found out about my overdraft, or the fact that I had been late in from the local coffee bar the previous night.

'I think you should know,' he said, drawing on his cigarette in his oddly elegant way, and speaking just as slowly as he always did, 'I think you should know,' he repeated, 'certain facts.'

I thought I was about to pass out with the horror of what was to come. Some months before he had already given me a long and very serious talk about the internal combustion engine; this might be going to be even worse. My stomach now actually resembled the internal combustion engine on a cold morning. However I knew not to interrupt his silences, or even his long pauses. Punishment came instantly if you did, in the form of his lowering his voice even more, and speaking even more slowly, which always made the backs of my knees ache with a kind of mixture of fear and impatience, rather like going down in a lift that was actually meant to be going up.

'The facts are rather delicate,' he continued, 'and you must promise not to pass them on.'

I stared at him. My best friend had already told me some Facts, on Bognor beach the previous summer, but of course I hadn't really believed her because, quite honestly, they didn't seem very nice, and certainly not the sort of things that people should be doing in their spare time. I actually said to her: 'If you believe that, you will believe anything.'

Now I stared at my father wondering whether to tell him what she knew, to save him trouble, and then wondering if that would matter, or count as 'passing them on'.

I was in such a state by now if I could have excused myself I would have done, but my father was not someone who encouraged people excusing themselves.

'The facts are these. Your mother knows them, and since you are of an age, now you are eighteen, she thinks you should know them too – but you must remember that from here on your lips are sealed, and you cannot tell anyone else.'

I didn't like to say that I would rather paint my toenails with poison than go around telling people things they either knew already or maybe didn't want to know, so I just resumed my young and innocent expression, which worked wonderfully well on other people; but my father was not other people, and as usual it had no effect, only seeming to make him look out of the window – probably trying to find something more interesting to look at than me and the drawing room.

'I work for MI5,' he announced.

'Oh, dear,' I said.

He returned his gaze to me. I had abandoned my young and innocent expression and swapped it in for startled daughter.

'What do you mean "oh, dear"?' he asked in an even more chilly tone.

'Well, it's not very nice, is it, MI5? It's full of people spying.'

He breathed in slowly, and out even more slowly. It was a sound that signified a thought that I knew must have occurred to him rather too often over my eighteen years of existence. Why, oh, why, God of all that is merciful, did you have to send me this daughter?

'As a matter of fact,' he conceded after a few seconds, 'you're right, MI5 is not very nice, and the reason it is not very nice is quite simple: we have to fight communism, and communism is not at all nice, and what is more we have to win, or we shall lose the very thing we have fought for during the war – our freedom.'

This was stern and strong stuff all right, but much as I didn't like the idea of having a father who was a spy,

6

at least it was better than the Facts of Life, and all those rather horrid things that a friend had told me on Bognor Beach.

'However, now you know, and you are sworn to secrecy, I must get on to the next subject, which is you.'

This was much better. I liked the idea of his changing the subject and getting on to me.

'It is time you got a proper job instead of drifting about in coffee bars and working for all sorts of people who your mother tells me she could never ask to dinner. So, I have made some enquiries and decided that the best place for you to work at a steady worthwhile job is – MI5.'

I stared at him in unbridled horror, there was no other way to describe the expression on my face. My expression was a hundred times worse than the way I'd looked on Bognor Beach the previous summer.

'What's the matter?' my father asked.

'I am not really suited to that kind of work,' I said, and realising that the young and innocent face hadn't worked, managed a slight sob in my voice.

'I think you are,' he said, with finality. 'And since you are a minor until you are twenty-one, there really is no point in arguing about it. I will get in touch with my people and they will make an appointment for you to go and see them. It is about time you settled down to doing something serious, patriotic, and worthwhile,

Lottie. Time to grow up. You are in danger of becoming a lightweight.'

I nodded silently and turned to leave the room. I liked being a lightweight, but of course I couldn't tell him that. Outside the sun was shining, but it might as well have been raining misery. Life as I had known it was about to be over. Life as I would like it to be was definitely not even on the horizon.

I turned back to face him.

'Of course, I don't suppose my typing and shorthand are up to their standards,' I said, suddenly feeling a great deal more cheerful.

'Don't worry, they'll soon shape you up,' came the reply.

I went upstairs to my room, and sat on the bed. It would be three years before I would be able to do as I wanted, before I reached that magical age of twenty-one when I could take up underwater diving, become a trapeze artist or a Great Painter. Then I brightened up. Maybe I would die before MI5 could shape me up? There was always that.

*

Quite an obvious thing to point out, but as it happened I didn't die. I did do my best to get pneumonia by standing in front of my bedroom window in a very thin nightdress and breathing in the cold night air for hours, but that didn't work. It is an unwritten law of the gods that if you are looking forward to something with all your heart and soul, you get ill, but if you try to be ill the gods just laugh at you and all you get is cold and bored.

Alas, my father must have tipped off the War Office to where I lived, same address as him – because in not a very short space of time the dreaded letter arrived inviting me to an interview.

I caught one of the vanishing number nines, as our local bus was called, and made my way to a very chic Mayfair address: the kind of house that used to be occupied by grand families for the summer season, when hunting stopped, and racing started. Disappointingly there were no cloaks or daggers hanging outside the front door, but inside the lift was rickety and old, and full of people at whom I tried not to stare, imagining they must all be spies, spooks or agents.

'You got our letter and the temporary pass all right?' asked the pleasant lady from behind her desk.

'I wouldn't be here otherwise, would I?' I asked brightly.

She gave a cold smile and I felt her unstated thought was, *We won't be having any more of that kind of cheek once you have signed the Official Secrets Act.*

Signing the Official Secrets Act turned out to involve answering a lot of questions that my father had told me the night before I could ignore if I wanted, because I was under his protection.

'Do you attend fashionable night clubs?'

I stared happily at that one. It could get me out of signing the wretched thing, get me out of being a part of the world of agents, spies and spooks that probably did go bump in the night. I wrote: 'I am a frequent visitor to night clubs, including the Blue Angel, and other clubs.' This took up more space than it should, which I hoped might also count against me.

I then put 'yes' beside all sorts of other questions that might portray me in an unsuitable light. By the time I'd finished ticking all the right boxes with all the wrong answers, I was convinced that the lady behind the desk would point to the door and invite me to leave. I might still be a minor, but there was nothing to stop me from being the wrong kind of minor. I felt almost gleeful as I handed her back my form.

She didn't even glance at it. I stared at her, appalled. What kind of organisation would take on someone like me? From the answers I had given, I was convinced I must be practically criminal. Certainly totally unsuitable to work for MI5.

But the truth was that she was not interested in anything except my shorthand and typing.

'I see that you have good speeds,' she said, staring approvingly at some of the references they had sent for.

'The Bullion Club has given you a very good reference. I didn't know it was still going, I used to go there with my brother, years ago. Bit of a clip joint, but excellent jazz.'

It was my turn to stare. She didn't look the type that would like jazz.

'I expect your father has explained everything to you? We will place you in a Section to work for a person of our choice, someone we think would suit you, and you would suit them. So, now all there is to do is get your security pass, and ask you to come back here at nine-thirty on Monday. I do hope you have a good weekend.'

Have a good weekend? How could I? I was about to become a sensible person with a proper job. Surely nothing could be worse? What was there now for me to look forward to? Nothing, except filing cabinets, shorthand and typing, and spooks in lifts wearing brown suits and matching shoes.

My mother was waiting for me when I got home. She looked at me in a baleful way. I always thought she could have got a university degree in baleful looks if she had wanted.

'Of course you can't go round dressed like that, and wearing two pairs of false eyelashes, if you're going to the Office,' she announced. 'No one can take shorthand properly through two pairs of eyelashes. I think we had better go shopping.'

My heart sank. Going shopping with my mother meant that she made friends with everyone in the dress department except me.

*

'Now that does suit you ... doesn't that suit her?'

I stared at myself in the dressing mirror. It was a suit all right, but the idea that it suited me was ridiculous. And then, with a feeling of dread, I realised something as the sales lady and my mother stood pulling at the skirt and tugging at the jacket. They were right.

The suit did suit me, it suited the me I was about to become: dull, grey, and conventional. Three years of being dull, grey, and conventional stretched ahead of me. Not so much a prison sentence, more like a life sentence.

It was time to put on a nightdress and stand in front of the open window again, hoping for pneumonia.

BEARDING THE DRAGON

Without my double false eyelashes I felt quite naked, which meant that when I was introduced to the Dragon to whom I had been appointed to work, my confidence was not at its highest.

I had sailed through security downstairs with my swanky MI5 pass, imagining that since the policemen on duty were so friendly, everyone else would be too, because my mother had a theory she often aired that if the doorman at a company was charming then so too would be the managing director. It was doubtless a sound theory in Civvy Street, but as the Dragon barked out her orders at me, I quickly realised that it might not be one that worked at MI5.

'No nail varnish in future, please, it only gets chipped on the typewriter keys and will make you look tarty.'

I wished yet again I were somewhere else with double pneumonia, or rather recovering from it.

'Oh, and I don't care for your makeup, young lady, and if those are false eyelashes you're wearing, take them off immediately.'

She leaned forward and for one awful moment I thought she was going to pull at my lashes.

'Actually they're mine,' I said, and pushed my chair away from her just in case she felt even tempted.

'Take a memo, please.'

And so started the first of a cascade of memos to do with people with strange names, who appeared to have attracted the wrong sort of attention to themselves. Every memo must be attached to a Personal File, and all to be typed up before lunch. I walked back down to the main room where all the secretaries worked, convinced I had probably made a hash of most of the memos. Entering the big room where it was rather obvious that only typewriters born on or before 1911 were permitted, I passed a tall, dark-haired girl also clutching files.

'Oh, you poor thing, you've got Dragon Dewsbury. She chews up secretaries for breakfast – a single comma out of place and she arranges for you to be shot at dawn. Meet you downstairs at one. Lunch at Fenwick's will cheer you up no end.' She stopped. 'I'm Arabella, by the way.'

'Lottie,' I said, trying to free a hand to shake hers with, and failing.

By the time lunchtime came I knew why the Dragon had earned her terrible reputation. It was true: one comma out of place meant that the whole memo had to be retyped, and since everything had to be backed up by triplicates of carbon paper, Fenwick's seemed to me not a shop but a heavenly haven, filled with enviably smart girls not tricked out in sensible grey, and not looking forward to an afternoon spent working for a dragon.

'The Dragon lost her fiancé in the war, and has never been nice to anyone since. Apparently.' Arabella paused, a forkful of salad waiting to be placed in her cupid's-bow mouth. 'The last girl who worked for her became so desperate she ran off with a married man who lives in Yorkshire – but that comes to the same thing really. Even so, you can see just how desperate she was.'

I gazed past Arabella for a few seconds. I imagined living in sin with a married man in Yorkshire where summer came and went in August, leaving the rest of the year to be cold and wet. I imagined eternally walking the moors, a wellie-booted reincarnation of Cathy from *Wuthering Heights*, lunch at Fenwick's an all-too-distant memory.

'What's your one like, is she a dragon too?' I asked.

Arabella gave me a look that told me at once I had asked a pathetic question.

'You are the first in and first out, new girl, that's why you got the Dragon. It's a short straw, a trial. If you can last a week with the Dragon, you can last a century with anyone else. Of course, there is a trick to it. The trick is to get her to move you out, but it's no good just doing rotten shorthand, because that means you won't get a reference. But there is something else you can do.'

Yes, but what? I wanted to know, and Arabella could see that without my asking. She sat back, knowing she had my complete attention.

'It was after the first hideous weeks in the Dragon's cave that I realised the way to slay her was to do what MI5 do to enemy agents.' Arabella looked suddenly proud. 'They find out their weaknesses, and then pursue them to the nth degree. The agents don't even know they're doing it. It's a bit like guerrilla warfare: so difficult to see where the enemy is coming from.' Her expression changed from one of pride to quiet glee. 'To begin at the beginning then. The Dragon can't stand the smell of garlic, but unlike with chipped nail varnish she can't tell you off about it. She hates the theatre, and actors – especially Richard Burton. In fact, she doesn't like Welsh people at all, and rugby football is next to sin in her view. She thinks television is an invention of the devil, and any mention of anyone on it – especially Sylvia Peters who did the Coronation – makes her go purple with fury. She thinks the Queen quite wrong to have appeared on it, and suspects that it was the Duke of Norfolk who talked her into it, because he is a Roman Catholic, and they are the source of all evil, past and present. She hates them, even more than she hates spiders.'

I was lost in admiration for Arabella. Well, who wouldn't be? The cleverness of her – to use the same techniques on the Dragon as MI5 used on enemy agents. What a fantastic coup.

'Anything more?' I asked hopefully, trying not to sound too enthusiastic.

'Oh, yes, one more thing. But you need to keep this one up your sleeve.' Arabella took a strawberry mousse from beside her place and centred it in front of her with the same elegant care I now realised that she did everything. 'In one name ...' she looked at me '... Noël Coward.'

I breathed in and out, slowly and happily. I loved Noël Coward with a passion. I could sing every song he ever wrote. I knew the first act of *Private Lives* off by heart, as well I should, since I had the LP recording of the Master playing Elyot and Gertrude Lawrence playing Amanda.

'This is wonderful. I know more about Noël Coward than anyone else does except his mother. So when should I start?' I asked, after a suitably long pause during which we finished our strawberry mousse.

Arabella put her head on one side, a habit I would soon recognise as being a signal for action.

'I think you should wait a day or two, and then start with the garlic. Do you have anything to do with the menus at home?'

I looked past her again. My mother was not someone who would encourage garlic. My father's taste in food was strictly English.

'I expect I can do something … perhaps. I'm not really allowed in the kitchen, not since I turned off the oven at Christmas.' As Arabella looked at me, I realised that further explanation was required. 'It had the turkey in it.'

'Harrods food hall has garlic now, but it is very expensive. You can go there, or to Covent Garden Market. If I still had some I would give it to you, but I used it all up on my mother's poodle.'

I already knew enough about Arabella not to ask her for an explanation as to why her mother's poodle had needed the same treatment as the Dragon. Arabella had about her a Gandhi-like aura. Her beautiful blue eyes had a gaze that seemed to be seeing something beyond what was happening at that moment. I instinctively knew she would not have wanted me to question her further. As the French say, she was not the one who would kiss – she was the one who would extend her cheek.

We returned to our Section, as I had learned that the large room organised for the secretaries was called. On the way we passed the files store. Arabella stopped in front of the goodly ladies who sat there, knitting and talking, surrounded by buff-coloured volumes, which were, I imagined, bulging with secret information. Of course it was not enough that Arabella knew everyone's name, she also knew about their knitting, which garment was for which child, or friend, and just how difficult it was to do cable stitching when people *would* come and ask for a PF or an SF.

'I don't know how they even get through a jumper let alone a cardigan,' she said, shaking her head as she went back to the desk that she had somehow managed to have placed opposite mine, our typewriters back to back, our telephones beside us, always on the alert for a call from our bosses.

My telephone rang. It was the Dragon, of course, wanting to dictate and spitting fire because she had just discovered a comma out of place.

Arabella nodded to me as I replaced the receiver.

'Just think garlic,' she said. 'It helps a lot.'

I did think garlic; I thought it so hard that by the time the Dragon had finished dictating at a wilfully terrifying speed, I was imagining myself breathing it all over her. That helped no end.

Back at home, it was a different matter. My mother heard my alarm clock going off at an ungodly hour and wanted to know why I was getting up at five in the morning when I didn't have to leave for the Office until eight-thirty. She found it deeply disturbing, as if I had taken up a new religion. She refused to let me leave. Going into London's Mayfair alone at such an hour was dangerous apparently. It was as bad as going out late at night. My father too did not find it in the least congenial. I lied to them that I wanted to go and sketch trees and bushes in Green Park before it got too crowded, but my father used his 'I know you're lying to me' voice, and I had to go into the garden and sketch a tree to prove that I wasn't. It was very chilly sitting on a sketching stool out there at that hour, and, worse than that, boring since there were only two very London trees and one bush.

*

'Your parents sound a bit like the Dragon.'

Arabella and I were back in Fenwick's lunching, and I was feeling a flop. She must have had a sixth sense because she rummaged in her handbag and brought out a bulb of garlic.

'I had to go to Harrods for my mother's nail-varnish order, so I bought you this. Can't have too much, I say.'

I felt touched, and to prove it I paid for both our lunches, but not before I had explained to Arabella that my parents were very, very strict, and there was nothing I could do about it until I was twenty-one, and not a minor any more.

'I'm lucky, I only have a mother. She sleeps a lot.' Arabella looked at me; her gaze was level. 'She sleeps with men. That's why I have to go to Harrods for her – she's always running out of makeup and stock-ings. She only goes to Hardy Amies for her clothes, and never Norman Hartnell because he made the Queen's wedding dress too heavy. Besides, Hardy Amies was very brave in the war, running around France spying. I know because my boss told me.' She paused, her eyes searching mine. 'Why do you think your parents are so strict?'

I frowned. It was difficult to explain.

'They're nice people,' I offered. 'But I don't think they ever liked children much. I think they had them because they thought they should, which is a bit like everything else that you think you should do: it never turns out to be much fun.'

Arabella considered this.

'My mother doesn't like children either. I once invited one home to tea, a child, a little girl belonging to our daily, and my mother kept moaning so much about her, as if she was a wild boar about to charge about the flat and break everything, that I had to take her to Fuller's Tea Room. Actually we had a whale of a time, and the cake was much better than anything we had at home, so it was just as well. I still take Doreen to tea there on Saturdays sometimes, but not on a regular basis, because that would lead to disappointment if I couldn't do it.' She stood up. 'Time to get back to dear Rosalie Browning. Such a sweetie. Do you know, for my sake, she dictates so slowly I practically fall asleep between sentences, but I daren't tell her. It would break her heart if she knew – she's that sort, always thinking of the other person – which is probably why she's never married.'

As I looked at her, wanting a bit more of Arabella's wisdom, she added, 'Men never marry *nice* women, they find them dull. Besides, Rosalie only really likes dogs. When she retires she is going to have dozens.'

Once back in the section I went to the loo and, summoning up my courage, carefully chewed a clove of garlic. A short pause later, filled with spite towards the Dragon, I carefully chewed two more.

Upstairs, after dictation, I leaned over her on pretext of seeing something – like a spider. One of those 'ooh, look' moments that children do when they want to pinch someone's biscuit. As I leaned over her I breathed hard over the Dragon. I waited for her to look sickened, or something, but she didn't.

'There is no spider,' she said in the furious tones that seemed to come so naturally to her. 'I think you need glasses as well as better shorthand.'

In a sudden moment of inspiration, and to make up for what I saw as the failure of the garlic, I assumed a devout expression and crossed myself.

'Thank God for that. I was sure I saw a spider as big as a tarantula,' I said in a pious voice.

The Dragon started breathing fire.

'There's no need to bring religion into it,' she said.

'Bless you,' I said, turning away and using an absent tone. 'And bless St Francis too for keeping the spider away from you.'

I could feel the Dragon staring after me, so much so that I thought I felt it all the way down the stairs until I arrived back at my desk.

'You're not looking happy,' Arabella stated.

I told her about the failure of the garlic.

'Give me the bulb,' she said calmly.

I fished into my handbag and fetched it out.

'There are three cloves missing,' she stated. 'Three cloves. Not one but three.'

'Yes,' I said, proud of my own courage. 'I chewed three.'

Arabella shook her head slowly.

'Don't you know the story about the Parisian model who couldn't give up garlic?' she asked in a kindly tone.

Of course I didn't know the story about the Parisian model who couldn't give up garlic.

'There had been nothing but complaints from clients at the Salon, where orders for clothes were given after she'd modelled them. She must give up garlic or lose her job, she was told. She returned home and, realising she could never give up using garlic, cooked roast lamb using, by way of rebellion, a dozen cloves of it. She ate the lamb, resigned herself to losing her job, and returned to the Salon. She modelled clothes all day for the richest of their clients – no complaints. She could not understand it until one of the seamstresses told her: masses of garlic, no smell; one little tiny piece and you stink.'

I returned home that night determined to give the garlic another trial. Just a little on my food every night, and the Dragon would be writing a memo to the Head of Section and I would be on my way to someone new. The idea of not having to take dictation from her was heaven on a biscuit, with or without garlic.

However what seemed simple on the number nine bus – top deck, front seat – was far from being so once I reached home. My mother was giving a dinner party for ten, and Mr and Mrs Graham were helping. They lived out, but came in to help about the place, and they were absolute dears, of course, always saying things like 'oh, Miss Lottie, you are such a wag', which sounded vaguely Shakespearean, but pleased me no end, because I am so egotistical. I never really questioned them as to what exactly a 'wag' was – and tonight was no exception since the guests were about to arrive.

Mr Graham was sent upstairs in his best suit to open the door and take coats, which he loved to do, and Mrs Graham was downstairs looking after the cooking.

'Gracious, this all looks so tempting, Mrs Graham,' I said, the halved clove of garlic in my pocket beginning to feel quite warm. My plan had been to lace one of the dishes, but Mrs Graham was hovering with intent.

'Your father says I am a wonderful cook,' she said with some satisfaction before she turned to look at me. 'I see from the placings that you're sitting between two of your father's business friends – that will be nice for you.' She gave me a look. 'Especially now you have a nice new regular job at the War Office.'

She gave me another look, and my heart sank. Never say that Mrs Graham knew about my father's work? Surely not? Were the Grahams too a part of the *ahem, ahem,* that must never be talked about? Did she know that I had signed the Official Secrets Act, which was now coming to seem to me far worse than knowing things that were sometimes talked about on Bognor Beach?

The clove of garlic was still in my pocket. It was beginning to feel like a hand grenade.

'You'll have to go and change, Miss Lottie. You know your father likes everything to be on the dot. He does not like us kept waiting on account of the last bus home. He is every inch a gentleman, every inch. And patriotic too, from the top of his head to the tips of his toes. My Stanley thinks he should be Prime Minister, he thinks that much of him.'

My father was always a feature of my conversations with the Grahams, and always would be. He was their hero, and when he was with them he became almost skittish, losing all his forbidding demeanour, laughing and joking with them in a way that he never did once he left the basement kitchen and went back upstairs to the drawing room. I had often noticed this. A while back, in an effort to get him to laugh, I had tried remembering jokes to tell him, and funny stories about things that had happened to me – or at least I thought they were funny – but they always fell rather flat, and for one reason or another, like it or lump it, it was only the Grahams who brought out his fun side.

As I ran upstairs to change I realised that my plan to lace one of the dinner dishes would have failed anyway, because the aroma of garlic floating about roast pheasant or spotted dick would have been sure to cause comment.

I rather dreaded dinners at home because I had to be so young at them. If I was with my friends in a coffee bar, or at Fenwick's having lunch, I could be old and wise for my years, but once among my father's and mother's friends, I had to become the kind of young woman-person they wanted me to be. Someone it had been worthwhile winning the war for. Even as I tried to sound girlish and nice, I always had a horrid feeling I was hardly worth winning a hockey match for. It was just a fact, and now that I knew it was perfectly possible that 'business friends' meant something quite other, I felt even more nervous and useless.

So there I was poised behind the drawing-room door, pinning on my best smile, when the first of my father's business friends arrived. I stared at them. They looked like business friends, they wore businessmen's suits, and they certainly talked like businessmen, but now I knew that, what with one thing and another, what with what I knew, and probably what they knew, they were quite likely to be agents. This notion had been somewhat enhanced by my father saying in a casual way after I had started working at MI5, 'A great many of the people who come to the house help me, but don't let that worry you.'

I had accepted this with something close to equanimity, until I realised that so many different people came to the house, they might all be agents, spies, or what Arabella called 'spooks'.

Dinner was a headache. First of all, although I had washed my hands and done what I could, the smell of garlic from my right hand was all too pervasive. When the man seated to the right of me sneezed, I was sure that it was not due to the white pepper he was liberally dusting his food with, but my garlic hand. 'The smell of the devil', Mrs Graham always called it, and no doubt he would think the same. I thought I should distract him with amusing conversation, and I think I managed to, because he laughed a lot, and since I couldn't tell him I worked at MI5, I told him all about the dreadful jobs I had done up until now, always hoping that he wouldn't ask the inevitable question.

'So what do you do now?'

I stared at him. I would have given a million pounds to say to him 'I work at MI5', and see him laugh and not believe me, but since I couldn't, I said, 'I work in a typing pool,' which was true.

His face fell.

'Someone as amusing as you should not work in a typing pool,' he said. 'I – I shall have a word with your father about this.'

'Oh, no, don't do that,' I pleaded with him. 'I haven't paid off my overdraft yet.'

'When you have, let me know and I will help you,' he said warmly, and as I left the table with the other ladies to join my mother at coffee, he turned and kissed my right hand.

It must have been the white pepper, but he truly didn't blench.

A CREDIT TO THE SECTION

My first four weeks at MI5 had gone by very quickly, probably due to the Dragon permanently breathing fire. Long memo after long memo came back with a single despising pen mark drawn through it.

'I can never believe she does that. Rosalie uses pencil so I can retype the mistakes and not do the whole thing again.' Arabella shook her head in disbelief. 'She really is unmitigated hell times two.'

I had to hand it to the Dragon: she was good at sadism. One of her tricks was to start speaking very, very slowly, so you were lulled into thinking that she was reforming her ways, only to find that this was not the case at all as she increased her speed little by little, ending up dictating so fast that even Mr Pitman would have trouble keeping up.

'Oh, dear, I keep forgetting your shorthand speed is only a hundred and twenty,' she would say with a sigh, after I had had to get in early to retype yet another clutch of memos and reports.

This particular day she looked across to the window, obviously remembering the halcyon days of her youth.

'I was a hundred and forty,' she said, with no attempt at modesty.

'You look much younger,' I murmured, crossing myself.

'We can do without jokes, Lottie, thank you. Our work is serious, we do not joke. Goodness knows, the world is insecure enough without jokes, what with the Atom Bomb, communism, and the wretched television.'

'I prayed for the security of the world at Mass this morning,' I told her.

The Dragon looked appalled.

'There is no need for you to do any such thing on my behalf, I do assure you,' she said, and for a second I could see she thought she could smell incense. There was a short pause while she chose her next line of attack. 'Really, I think you should keep to the rules here in the Section – unwritten though they may be. We do not mention religion or politics.'

'My father mentions religion sometimes. He said Roman Catholics were allowed into MI5 now, on account of the fact they hate communism so much.'

'Your father is a very distinguished man,' the Dragon said shortly.

Perhaps the mention of a more senior officer tempered her attitude because for the rest of the day she did not ring me for dictation, which meant that I was left kicking my heels downstairs among the dreary green filing cabinets. It was their very dreariness that gave me an idea.

In my lunch hour I bought some magazines and Sellotape and cut out some pictures of movie stars, which I taped on to the front of the cabinets.

I put Cary Grant alongside Grace Kelly, then Elizabeth Taylor and Marilyn Monroe, last but not least.

'Do admit they cheer the place up?'

'You'll probably end up in the Tower for doing that,' Doreen the arch knitter from Files said when she saw my handiwork. 'But I tell you, that is what MI5 needs: a bit of movie-going magic. Good for you.'

The rest of the Section stared at my work in silent fascination.

'Not so dismal now, are they, these awful cabinets?' I asked, looking round at the rest of them.

There was the sound of jaws dropping all around the room as, one by one, everybody took in my artwork. I could not say that they approved. They were too shocked to be able to approve. I suddenly knew how Manet felt at the first showing of his masterpiece Le Déjeuner sur l'herbe, the painting that rocked Paris. But like Manet I resolved to stand by my creation. I would not take any notice of lesser mortals with their petit-bourgeois attitudes.

Arabella approved of my artwork.

'Someone should have done that years ago,' she murmured before putting on her intercept headphones, a dreamy look coming into her eyes.

'How's it going?' I asked, glancing up from my book as there was still no sign or sound of the Dragon and her doings.

'It' was the raging affair that was being conducted by a well-known and very active member of the British Communist Party and an obviously extremely virile gentleman whose daytime occupation was working as a ticket collector at Earl's Court Underground station.

'She is taking him to dinner tonight, and then they're going back to her flat for a coffee,' Arabella whispered, because she was really meant to be typing, not listening.

'And then what?'

'Who knows? I don't think she does. She can't ... she keeps saying she feels faint at the sound of his voice.'

'Why are they interesting?'

'Because he's a double agent, silly.'

I must admit up until then, what with the long and boring memos and trying to cope with the Dragon, I had forgotten that MI5 was all about catching communists.

'What happens once they've caught one?' I asked Arabella later, over tea in the canteen.

'How do you mean?'

'Well, they survey someone, say, and they find out they are red through and through, so what then? I mean this chap you listen to, he comes back and tells someone here "Yes, you're right, she is a communist", which let's face it, they know already, and then what happens?'

Arabella looked mystical.

'I don't know. I daresay they make the communist's life hell,' she said.

'What, let down their tyres, and put dye in their laundrette bag when no one is looking?' A dreadful thought occurred to me. 'They don't drug them and send them to – to Russia, do they?'

'Gracious, no, there is no point in sending them to Russia. There are quite enough communists there already, no point in adding to them. No, I'm not sure what they do, but I am quite sure they menace them. You know – pile on the tax bills, listen in to their telephones, follow them wherever they go ... restaurants, cinemas, theatres, parks ... especially parks, apparently.'

I was not satisfied, but Arabella had centred her teacake in front of her place, and once that happened I knew to pipe down until she had cut it into as many tiny slices as she could before tenderly delivering them to her mouth.

'It sounds to me ...' I said finally, half to myself ' ... it sounds to me as if catching communists is a bit of a waste of time. I mean, you catch them – that is, you know who they are – and then you follow them week in, week out, to make sure that they're not doing anything terrible besides reading the *Daily Worker*. I just don't see how that can be much use in the defence of our country. What are they doing that is so wrong?'

'They are doing wrong things, all the time. They're busy making people strike, sewing seeds of anarchy, bringing transport to a standstill, crippling our exports. Rosalie says they could put the whole country out of action, just bring it to a standstill, if they were better organised, and that is what Russia wants, and other countries too. They can't wait to take the Great out of Britain. So that is what we are here for: to make their life unmitigated hell. But in a very nice way, of course, because that is what we British do. We make people suffer in a nice way, and then make sure they stop being stupid and realise being a nuisance is not on.'

I stared at Arabella. She had obviously had a lot of thoughts about MI5 and all that, and also come to quite a few rather good conclusions. She had made me feel less grey, and more excited about our work. Catching a communist spy who was buying secrets from us was going to be fun, and also patriotic. It might even mean that the number nines would be more frequent.

I waltzed back into our Section feeling pretty chipper.

It was only as I passed Files that I noticed they were unusually quiet, as was the rest of the room. Everyone was busy being Very Busy as if they had all been told not to look at me.

I went to my desk and looked around. Still no one was looking at me. I didn't like that, I like people looking at me, but worse than that there had been skulduggery at work – the decorations on the filing cabinets had been removed.

The telephone on my desk rang. I picked up, knowing that nothing good was going to come of answering this call and being proved instantly right.

'Please will you come down to the first floor? Head of Section wants to see you at once.'

I put down my handbag, knowing that it might be the last time it was left on my desk. I turned to Arabella, who was once more listening enthralled to her intercept, but seeing the look on my face, she put down her earphones.

'You have the look of someone who has just heard something beastly,' she said.

'I have to go down to the first floor. Head of Section wants to see me.'

Arabella looked serious.

'The first floor is where they – but, well, I mustn't say.'

'Where they what?'

'You will find out soon enough.'

'No, tell me.'

'I can't. It's classified information. You have to show your pass three times just to get through to whoever is seeing you, so don't be surprised at what happens. It's torture.'

'Torture?'

'Torture, but you'll come through it, because you're so plucky. Really, you will. Just don't say too much. No matter what, say as little as you can.'

I gave her my best 'it's a far, far better thing I do now' look, which was completely wasted on her as she was back listening to the double agent wooing the communist lady.

Down, down I went, I thought, just like Richard II, 'wanting the manage of unruly jades' – a line that always comes to my mind in certain circumstances simply because it is about the only one I can remember from *Richard II*. As a matter of fact, I really would have given anything to be on a bolting horse rather than the knee-knocking experience of showing my security pass three times, and trying out my best smile on three different door Johnnies, who looked intensely bored by seeing both me and my pass, so there was no point in trying to charm them.

Finally I came to Head of Section's door. I knew it was the right door because it said *Head of Section* on it.

As I went in I remembered Arabella's reassuring words about the British not torturing people; even so

I looked around me straight away. There was no sign of anything except bookshelves.

'How are you, young lady?'

It wasn't the same lady who had let me in, as it were. This one was very different. I thought she must be grander, because she had a better desk and a Parker pen, and I had passed two secretaries on the way in.

I went to say 'I am quite well, thank you' but I couldn't get the words out, so I just stood and waited, dreading to hear what kind of agonies I was going to have to endure for putting up the pics of movie stars on the filing cabinets.

'Do sit down.'

I sat down.

'I expect you know why you're here?'

I nodded, already a broken reed, awaiting my sentence.

She opened a file and read through it.

'Four weeks,' she finally stated. 'You have been here four weeks, and already you are, I believe, a credit to your Section.'

I stared at her. Was it possible that this was a refined MI5 kind of torture? They led you to believe one thing, before twisting it in such a way that you were forced to confess to something you had never done? Anything was possible. I knew that my father was very good at laying traps, because I had more than once fallen into one.

'Yes, your work has been satisfactory. You are quite prepared to correct your mistakes, and more than that – you always have a cheerful mien.'

I never quite knew what a 'cheerful mien' was but now I realised that I was supposed to have one, I immediately assumed an expression of life-enhancing goodwill.

She looked at me with sudden concern.

'Are you feeling all right?'

'Definitely, thank you.'

'Oh, good, you seemed to have lost colour.'

'Oh, I'm always losing things. It's just a habit.'

She laughed.

'I can see why you're such an asset to your Section, yes indeed.'

She paused. 'So, now you can go home to your father and tell him that you have passed our requirements, and what is more we are very pleased with you.' She paused again. 'I know you will go on to even greater things, but for the time being I am only too happy to leave you in your present position, where you are giving so much satisfaction.

'For the first year your weekly wage will remain the same, but you get six weeks' paid leave, as it is known here, which I always think is such an asset, truly. You can take the whole six weeks as one, if you wish, which means that you can, say, go to Ascot and follow the Season a little, if you like, or you can take off to warmer climes and sizzle on the beaches. But for now – thank you for coming to see me, and well done. Very well done indeed. Most pleased.'

I walked back to the door, painfully aware that my legs felt weak and my head quite light.

Her voice stopped me as I reached for the door handle.

'Just one more thing.'

I turned, knowing that the Real Truth was about to be spoken and that she had been leading me on.

'Yes, just one thing, and I am sure you won't mind my mentioning it. Best if you don't try decorating the filing cabinets again. Might lead to an outbreak of travel posters and pin ups. Such a nice thought though, nonetheless.'

'Of course. Thank you.'

I floated past the policemen, proudly flashing my security pass, and then took the lift back to what I now thought of as My Floor. I had passed my month's trial at MI5. My work was satisfactory. I hadn't been tortured. I walked into the Section, and went straight up to Arabella.

'It was fine. Just my first month assessment.'

Arabella looked innocent.

'I thought it might be. So...' She looked at me with her most sanguine expression. 'You'll be staying on with the Dragon then? What fun.'

I stared at her. I hadn't thought about that. It meant, instead of being shot of her, I was cemented into position. If I could have made my eyes fill with tears, I would have done, but as it was time to get back on the number nine bus, I couldn't afford that luxury. I should go and find out what was happening at home, because now I Knew What I Knew, it seemed to me that something always was.

THE FASTEST GUN IN W8

I had always found it difficult to understand why my mother perpetually had people in the house, either calling or staying, but now I knew that they were probably all spies and spooks and agents of one kind or another, it was quite understandable.

That evening, after I had stopped for a coffee with Arabella, I wandered home, happy in the knowledge that my mother would be only too pleased to hear that I had passed into the inner sanctum of MI5 and would be earning eight pounds a week, and enjoying six weeks' holiday on full pay. I knew she would like that last bit so much because it would mean I would be somewhere else rather than sitting about the house, which the previous evening she had told me she found a bit much because I was taking up a room that she would prefer to use for guests. She hinted now, almost daily, that my moving out might be much the best course for both of us.

For this reason I found myself putting my front-door key in the latch and creeping into the house as if I were on a spying mission, which I knew I wasn't, but even so it seemed a better way to enter, quietly, surreptitiously, without causing a stir. As I crept past the drawing-room door, I could not help but glance in – just to make sure of the numbers at dinner, I told myself, but really it was because I wanted to know who might be there. My father was, but not my mother. My father was having a long, quiet conversation with a man in one corner of the room, while the other people present, a mixed lot, were talking to each other in a desultory way, as if they were all awaiting the result of my father's conversation with the gentleman in question.

I climbed the stairs to my room, passing the door of one of the guest rooms on the way. I paused. I could hear someone moving about inside. As quietly as possible, in the same way I had opened the front door, I pushed open the guest-room door, only to stop. I was right; there was someone in the room. It was my mother and she was holding a gun.

My first thought was that I had to move out, straight away. I mean, if this was what it had come to, there was no question. For once in my life I found there were no words I could think of that were appropriate to the situation. I knew at once from Mother's expression that making a joke was just not on. She had a very cross look on her face, so cross that it reminded me of the day I pulled some bobbles off the curtain trimming in her bedroom. It was that bad.

'I have told your father time and time again,' she said, moving the gun about as she talked in a way that would make a grown man faint, 'he is not to leave revolvers in the side drawer of the guest rooms. He will do it. It is bad enough he goes around with a knuckleduster in his pocket, pulling his suit out of shape, bad enough that his swordstick came apart at the races the other day, but now here we are with guns where they definitely should not be. If only he wasn't so absent-minded.' She sighed. 'It takes a terrible toll on the wives, all this undercover business, what with weapons, and people coming and going at all times of the day and night – including your father, one never knows where he is – and now guns in awkward places. I mean supposing Mrs Graham had found it, or your grandmother – particularly your grandmother – she would have a fit.'

I saw my opportunity to open up the conversation a bit. After all, from my understanding of the Grahams, they were working for my father anyway and a gun here or there might not make any difference, I shouldn't have thought.

'I expect Mrs Graham would understand,' I offered. 'Besides, she doesn't look in drawers. She only dusts.'

My mother threw me a pitying look, which although it was less terrifying than her previous expression, was still not exactly cordial.

'Everyone looks in drawers, it is just a fact, and if you don't know that then you should. Everyone looks in drawers, handbags, envelopes and medicine cabinets, just so long as it is nothing to do with them. People feel compelled to look. That's just a simple fact. On the other hand, if it is to do with them, they will no more glance in a drawer, look in their handbag, open an envelope or even a medicine cupboard, unless they absolutely have to. That is human nature, Lottie, and if you don't know it by now, then you should do.'

She looked at the gun, which was still in her hand.

'I don't know if it is loaded,' she said crossly. 'You had better go down and ask your father.' She sighed again. 'He's having one of his bogey dinners, no one allowed except him and his inner bogey circle.' She shook her head once more. 'And that is another thing that is so dull about being married to someone in the security service – it makes socialising so difficult. How can I keep up my social life in any kind of way when I can never count on your father being there? And if he's not there, he's some-where else doing something most wives would rather not know about. Really, it is impossible. If I could, I would get in touch with the Director Generals of both services and point this out to them. The strain on the wives' social lives – and, believe me, it is a strain – is terrible.'

She frowned and indicated with the revolver that I should leave.

'Go and find your father and ask him if this dreadful thing is loaded or not,' she repeated. 'And if so does he want to unload it, or does he want me to put it back for some luckless person to find it?'

It wasn't difficult to leave the guest room, but as I went downstairs I have to say I found it in me to feel very sorry for my mother. I could see her point of view. There obviously was no social life that she could count on, what with spies and spooks, and dinner parties for what she called 'bogeys' where she wasn't wanted. It was hard for her. She was sacrificing a lot for her country, for the fight against communism. Even so, sidling into the drawing room to find my father and ask him if the revolver he had absentmindedly left in a drawer was loaded, was not the easiest thing to do.

'*Psst?*'

He looked at me.

'*Psst* to you too,' he said briefly.

'No, really, *psst,* you know proper *psst*, not pretend *psst*,' I whispered to him.

It was a noise I used to make when I was little to alert him to my grandmother coming to the front door. It had always worked like magic. At the thought of the imminent arrival of his mother-in-law my father, who never, ever moved fast, could suddenly sprint faster than the speed of sound.

'Up the wooden stairs to Bedfordshire,' I said, jerking my head towards the stairs.

'What are you talking about, Lottie?'

He was beginning to look ruffled.

'I am talking about the toy you left in the side drawer in the guest room, Daddy,' I said, winking and blinking in a way that I hoped he was used to with his spooks. 'Someone has found it and is playing with it, and she thinks it might be loaded, which toy guns shouldn't be, she thinks.'

Once again my father demonstrated just how fast he could move when it was necessary.

I followed him upstairs, but very slowly, to allow for harsh words and maybe a gunshot or two.

'You must not worry about this sort of thing, my dear,' I heard my father saying. 'Of course the gun is loaded, but the catch is on, so there's no need for concern. As long as the safety catch is on, nothing can happen. Stand away, dear.'

Following this there was the sound of a catch being put on, and my mother making the kind of noise that women tend to make when they see a mouse.

I could stand it no longer and fled to my room where I lay down on my bed and wished that communists would behave themselves so that my mother could have a social life and my father needn't go around with knuckledusters pulling his suits out of shape, and swordsticks that fell apart at the wrong moment, and guns that popped up in awkward places.

I should have liked it if my life could have returned to what nice people would call normal, but now I was part of the inner circle that surrounded my father, I had a feeling that it was not going to be possible.

Life in the Section was as normal as blueberry pie compared to life at our house. I envied all the other girls the fact that their fathers did not go about cloaked in secrecy. Their fathers did things like go to the City and earn pots of money while my father went about preventing Britain from descending into anarchy. Their fathers bought Jaguar cars, and went to their tailors for smart suits, whereas, my father explained to me, for his work he must not look anything out of the ordinary. He must wear off-the-peg suits and drive a dull car, so as not to be noticed more than the next man. It was a sacrifice for him, as he readily now acknowledged, because as he said he liked what he called 'flash' things, and being a great admirer of the Romans, he told me that there was nothing he would have liked more than to wear a toga and gold arm-bands, but that was just not possible, given his line of work.

'A great deal of my work takes me to places where some sort of smart alec would be noticed immediately,' he told me the following week when we were having lunch together in what my mother called 'his bogey hotel'. It was the place where he always conducted business outside the Office. The waiters greeted him as a long-lost friend, which was a bit unusual, I thought, until I realised that judging from their accents they must all of them hail from behind the Iron Curtain. 'It is very hard on your mother, I know, going around in a nondescript motor car with a man in a dingy mackintosh, but she understands that sacrifices must be made.'

I tried to look cheerful about the sacrifices that must be made by my mother, all the while thinking that it was a bit much. Maybe married men should not work in MI5? Maybe they should only have bachelors working there.

'Oh, don't worry, we have quite a few bachelors,' my father told me shortly. 'And quite a few friends of Dorothy too.'

'Does she work in my Section?' I asked in a low voice.

'You should know who works in your Section, Lottie. And anyway, that's not what a friend of Dorothy's means. But that is not why you are here.'

He paused to light a cigarette.

'The reason you are here is so that I can run through a few things with you. First of all ...' He took off his glasses and looked grimly serious, and seriously grim, both at the same time, which he was very good at.

Looking at him, I felt almost as nervous as I had before showing my security pass three times and going in to see Head of Section.

'First of all,' he went on, 'you must never, ever acknowledge me when I am out.'

I nodded, and then thinking that I should make a contribution, said, 'Is it because of your suits?'

He breathed in and out very slowly, just as my mother always seemed to do when talking to me. I seemed to have that effect on them.

'The suits do come into it,' he acknowledged. 'You have probably noticed that today, for instance, I am in Savile Row suiting, and that is because I am being me, here with you, whereas if I were out and about on business, I would be in off-the-peg, and even a shabby mackintosh.'

'Yes, of course.'

Actually I hadn't noticed at all. In fact not noticing my father had become something of a habit ever since I once rushed up to him, thinking he was waiting to collect me from the school train, and quite unable to believe that he was, had greeted him enthusiastically, only to be pushed away and told 'I am not your father', which had the effect of making me believe I was adopted, only to be told by my mother – to my intense disappointment – that I was not.

'That was just your father's idea of a joke,' she said vaguely, adding, 'he can be very funny like that.'

I knew he was not being funny now, so as we left his bogey hotel I practised not knowing him. As he walked away I imagined that he was someone else, but it was difficult because he was walking very slowly, and smoking, and hailing a taxi, and I thought he was probably going back home to change into a shabby mackintosh and that seemed a pity because he looked really rather smart over lunch, and I would have liked him to have been driving off in an equally smart Jaguar car like other girls' fathers did, but he was determined on winning the battle against communism, and making sure that people could do what they wanted, unlike communists who seemed to spend the whole time sending people to Siberia for writing poems.

'Did you have a nice lunch?' the Dragon wanted to know later when I went up for dictation.

I nodded, but I know I looked evasive, because she stared at me.

'Lunch with your father must be fun,' she went on. 'He is always joking and laughing in his Section, his secretary told me. He is the life and soul of it.'

It was my turn to stare at the Dragon.

So I was right. My father could only laugh and joke with spies and spooks and agents, and such like, people like the Grahams and those people in the drawing room. I remembered laughter coming up from the dining room during his 'bogey dinner', and my mother saying: 'That's another thing. I'm never allowed to know what they're laughing at. Really it is too hard.'

Of course it was, but not as hard as being sent to Siberia for writing a poem.

A BUNGLARY

My mother was looking at me so intently that I feared I had put on the wrong shoes, or forgotten that I mustn't wear false eyelashes any more, no matter what.

'I wish that you were not caught up in all this,' she said in a matter-of-fact way. 'It is bad enough that you are at home, and rather in the habit of getting under everyone's feet. But now you are coming home with secrets and facts that I don't want you to talk about, and you probably couldn't talk about anyway, even if you wanted. This means that there are not just bogeys in the drawing room all the time, but now my own daughter is one too. If only you had been able to get another sort of job, but you would keep on being sacked, and that is just hopeless. If you are sacked too many times people start to think there is something wrong with you, and let's face it, Lottie, there must be if you couldn't even hold down a job in a coffee bar on a Sunday evening. You only lasted three hours at the *Italiano*, and besides its not being remotely suitable, it was even less suitable once you had been there.'

Some weeks before a friend had found me a job for a few hours a week in a coffee bar in Knightsbridge. Just newly opened, it had something called a Gaggia coffee machine. Everyone else seemed to work it all right. In fact it was generally considered to be quite simple – that is until I moved in on it, and it became a coffee version of the Dragon on a bad day, spitting frothy milk – not that the Dragon did that, but sometimes it seemed that she very well might – and pouring black coffee too fast into a cup that was too small.

'That was a bit too much for me, I admit,' I agreed. 'I am not handy. In fact, if you were going to be calling me anything, you would call me unhandy. More than that – you would call me cack-handed.'

'And I don't think we want that sort of language, thank you,' my mother said, trying to look offended when we both knew perfectly well that having been in the Wrens during the war, she knew several bad words.

'Is there something wrong?' I asked, making a rather lame attempt at being sensitive and friendly.

My mother sat down suddenly, which was awkward because she was sitting between me and my bedroom door and I was longing to escape so that I could go to the kitchen and make myself a hot drink.

'Your father has gone out on a burglary,' she confessed, suddenly, 'and it does not bode well. I am really rather afraid for him. If he gets caught by the police, it could be a little embarrassing.'

I stared at her.

My father's life seemed altogether colourful enough without his having to turn to burglary.

'Have the bills mounted up that much?' I asked in what I hoped was a tender and tactful way.

'Oh, no – this has nothing to do with bills,' she said, tetchily. 'No, no, this is to do with information stored in other people's private houses, address books and so on, things that would be of no interest to anyone except your father. Not that he is nosy,' she added quickly. 'No, this is because he needs to know what they know, even though it is probably useless, but that is what spying is all about.'

'Has he done this before, this burglary business?'

'Oh, yes, many times, but this is different.' She looked at me. 'The thing is – he has often gone burgling before, but this time the house he is breaking into belongs to *friends* of ours.'

I stared at her.

'But you can't break into friends' houses. It just isn't on,' I protested.

'Exactly how I feel,' my mother agreed. 'But it seems that they may have pretty dreadful links with people behind the Iron Curtain or somewhere like that, and they may be very, very clever at pretending to be the kind of people we are – when they're not at all.'

I knew at once what she was not saying and probably wouldn't dare to say, even to me.

'I don't know how anyone gets from A to B when it comes to security,' she went on. 'I mean, potentially everyone is a double agent, and now it seems it can only be proved by breaking into people's lovely homes and going through their things. I mean it is the most awful notion, but what can you do about it?'

'Would you like a cup of hot chocolate?' I asked because it was usually my answer to everything.

'Yes, that would be nice,' she said, and we went downstairs to the kitchen and made hot chocolate, only to be disturbed a very little later by my father and another man, returning really rather noisily and not at all like I imagined burglars should.

'We almost got caught, my dear, just as you said we might be,' my father announced triumphantly as we came upstairs and met them in the drawing room.

'Luckily Roger here had the presence of mind to call the police.'

As my mother stared at them my father explained.

'We broke in all right. The skeleton keys worked perfectly, and we took some snaps, but then you-know-who came back much earlier than expected because they found the opera tedious and left in the interval – so Roger sprang to the telephone and called 999, while I explained that we had been passing the house when we realised the front door was ajar and there were people inside intent on burglary.'

He started to laugh.

'They were so grateful. Really they were. Particularly, they said, since nothing had been taken, thank goodness.'

I tried to laugh and my mother tried to laugh, and we went to bed only too thankful that nothing more had happened.

But my feeling of relief did not last long. The following day Arabella told me I had been appointed to Security Codes and Safes.

We all had our individual codes to our individual safes, but the main safe had them all. He was Top Top Safe, so very safe.

'It's a two-week rota,' she explained. 'You just have to be the first in and the last out. Quite simple, nothing to it, we've all done it, and you'll get the hang of it in a second.'

I couldn't agree with her. Memories of the Gaggia machine came back to me, the faces of the customers as they surveyed hot milk instead of coffee, and coffee instead of tea, this coupled with the face of the proprietor when I told him that I had waived any payments from the customers because I felt so bad about it all – the memories were not at all reassuring. The proprietor had not been pleased, but he was not a member of MI5; he had merely entrusted me with his Gaggia machine, and the result had been spillage of a high order, but not war with Russia. Now I was being entrusted with security files, and codes for all the cabinets, the final one that only I could know being changed every week and being Top Secret, which was the highest rating.

Arabella ran through the whole process for me several times.

'The main safe clicks in the same way that your personal safe clicks each way you turn it,' she said, using her helpful voice. 'You know, turn it to the right, click, turn it twice to the left, click, click, and so on. Well, it is the same principle with the main safe. You will be given a code and none of us will know it, click, click, click, and all our codes will be in there, and the same for the door, click, click, click.'

I wished to goodness she would stop clicking at me, I was beginning to find it unnerving, a bit like being faced with a clucking hen, but with no nice egg in prospect.

'I don't suppose anyone will be later than you tonight,' she added, 'because I suspect the Dragon will be up to her usual tricks and you will have to redo a whole lot of work, so it won't be too much bother for you to stay on.'

It seemed to me that there was nothing quieter at evening-tide than MI5.

Of course I did indeed have a whole lot of work to redo, but the sound of the old Underwood I was typing on was like a hammer banging in my head. I stopped every now and then, wondering what I would do if the Section were broken into.

Supposing a Russian armed to the teeth, and knowing that I was my father's daughter, had prior knowledge of my being in charge of Section Codes and broke in and demanded the Big Code for the central safe?

I wished that I had my father's knuckleduster, but then I realised that it would be far too big for my hand and wished for his swordstick instead. I could run someone through all right ... but then I set to wondering if I really could.

Maybe the gun would be better? But would it be worth it? Killing a man intent on trying to find out about communists might be a bit of a waste of time since he was one himself. This thought made me relax. I would not be responsible for ending someone's life, but I might ask him to sit down and would make him a nice cup of tea on the sound principle that this was the British way.

I glanced at my watch. It was late all right, and no one else was in the Section. I must now do this very simple thing. I must shut up my safe as I always did, and go to the main safe, remembering the secret code, click, click, click it in, and then go home satisfied that I had done my duty to Her Majesty's government, Great Britain and democracy.

I said goodnight in a cheerful manner to the policeman on the door, and sashayed down the street to the bus stop, filled with the confidence of a person who has done a job well. As luck would have it fortune smiled on me. A number nine came trundling up.

The bus conductor sang tunefully. I sat in my favourite seat watching London on a spring evening from the top deck, and thought of all the things that I would do when I reached home. I would go quietly to my room, taking with me something to eat, which I would wheedle out of Mrs Graham, and then I would lie down on my bed and read one of my favourite books.

Everything was fine until I reached home. It was just as I was putting my key in the lock that I realised I had shut the main safe, but had I remembered to shut my own? I simply couldn't recall doing so.

I stood on the pavement outside the house, trying and trying to recall the wretched sequence of events, until I decided there was nothing else to be done except to go back. If I couldn't remember whether I had closed my own safe, perhaps I hadn't even closed the main safe? I hurried back down the front steps to the road and started to run. No good waiting for the bus – by the time it arrived the dreaded masked Russian raider of my imagination could have purloined the secrets of the whole Section. I took a taxi back to MI5. Once there I sprang out of the cab and rushed inside.

The policeman on the door gave me a patronising smile. I did not like it at all. I bolted back up to our floor, and skidded to a halt in the main room. Hardly able to put one foot in front of the other, I wobbled up to my safe. It was locked all right. I turned to the main safe. Remembering all the numbers, I reopened it. Everything that should be in there was in there. I relocked it using the right combination, and then I sat down for a few seconds. I had done it right. I could hardly believe it, but then I remembered the one thing that Arabella had told me – never, ever to lock any safe without turning back to it and saying out loud: 'I have locked the safe.' I had been so busy being irritated by her clicking at me, I had forgotten the golden rule.

I staggered past the policeman on the door. He gave me another patronising smile.

'Forgot the golden rule? They always do, the new ones,' he murmured.

I said nothing in reply. I had no money left in my purse. Happily it was a warm evening. I walked all the way home, and since I was so tired it took a long, long time to reach my parents' house. When I did, having no appetite for anything else, I went up to my bedroom and lay down on my bed.

It would be the last time I didn't listen to Arabella.

'Well,' she said the next day, realising from my extreme pallor and my weary tones that all had not been well the night before, 'at least you only had to come back from Kensington. That poor thing over there,' she nodded across the room at a figure bent over her typewriter, 'her first night on Security Safe, she had to come back from Basingstoke. Basingstoke! I mean, can you imagine?'

I could not imagine. Gracious, Kensington had been bad enough.

'No last buses,' Arabella went on, obviously determined to make me feel sympathetic to the luckless girl across the way, which was rather annoying when all I wanted to feel was sorry for myself. 'No bus to take her home so she had to walk the fifteen miles to her mother's cottage, by which time she had pneumonia.'

'Pneumonia's very difficult to get,' I said with some feeling.

'Well, a cold then,' Arabella conceded.

So now what? I wondered. Another ten days shouting at the Top Secret safes 'I have done your codes, so you can't deceive me again'? Suddenly it was too quiet, and more than that the Dragon was dictating very, very slowly, and not speeding up at all towards the end. I was worried, and I was not the only one. Like most people who breathe fire if not brimstone at every turn, the Dragon was expected to continue behaving in a familiar pattern, but she wasn't and to be truthful I was worried. She was walking more slowly, the air was not filled with fury whenever she saw a comma out of place, she had even suggested it would be nicer for me if she used a pencil to correct anything that was wrong with my typing, and no further memos came back down the stairs to the section with a bold inked line through them. Even Arabella noticed.

'I don't think she's well,' she said, and looked both solemn and mystical at the same time, which was a special quality that Arabella and only Arabella could exude. It was as if she was not sitting on a typing chair in front of an old Underwood, but poised Gandhi-like on nails and oblivious to whatever was happening around her, while at the same time exuding a kind of goodness that would help to cure the ills of anyone passing by. It was an extraordinary quality, and I wished so much that I could have it too, but the truth was I was sadly lacking in any natural serenity.

'What shall I do?' I asked, a little helplessly, while feeling the terrible guilt that overwhelms anyone who thinks they have been beastly about someone who is not well.

'I will tell Head of Section that she should see the M.O.,' Arabella said, quietly, and of course serenely. She stood up and carefully pushed her chair in. 'Rosalie said something must be done before she went on leave, but she forgot to say what.'

Sometime later Arabella came back into the Section. She still looked serene, but pale.

'The Dragon has collapsed,' she said, shortly. 'Security have had to call an ambulance.'

I pulled back the yellowing lace curtain that hid MI5 from the rest of the world, and watched in silence as indeed an ambulance pulled up and a stretcher bearing the Dragon disappeared within. Suddenly she seemed very sad and frail, and I felt dreadful. Suppose my attempts at annoying her with garlic and Roman Catholicism and snatches of Noël Coward songs had added to her ill health? Worse – suppose they had even caused it?

I went home feeling at a loss, as is only natural when you find yourself without a wall to bang your head against.

Later my father came in and told me that it was peritonitis.

'She is a game old thing. I'm sure she'll pull through,' he said, absently, his mind on other things.

I didn't go along with this, so I prayed hard for the Dragon that night. I prayed in the only way I knew how, in the 'please, God, help the Dragon to get better' kind of way, because those were the only prayers I knew really. Arabella too was praying, but she was more organised with her prayers, saying masses of Our Fathers, she told me, making sure that I knew.

Next day I went into MI5 bright and early, hoping against hope that the Dragon news was going to be good. I missed her. My telephone was all too silent. I looked at the files she had prepared for me in previous weeks, and even missed her bold inky lines swiping through some hapless memo.

Rosalie returned from leave, and we all decided to send the Dragon some flowers. She was at King Edward VII's Hospital for Officers, and the news was that she was recovering.

'Do you think she would like us to visit her?' I asked Arabella.

Arabella thought for a minute.

'If we don't stay too long and don't eat all the Newbury Fruits we're going to take her, I think she would probably like it.'

I had never thought of the Dragon as a human being before, but now that she was sitting up in bed, pale but determined, wearing a pink angora bed jacket, I saw all too clearly she really was an actual human being.

'We won't make you laugh, I promise,' Arabella began, 'because of your stitches.'

The Dragon smiled, and it was a warm, kind smile, which transformed her whole face.

'You have been through a dreadful time,' I put in. 'And I'm not just talking about having me for a secretary.'

Her hands slid down the counterpane to where her stitches must be as she tried not to laugh.

'One thing I must tell you,' she said, her expression still gentle and kindly. 'Rosalie said that you were both praying for me, and it was that thought that brought me through. I've never thought too much of Papists, on account of the Gunpowder Plot, but now I believe I've changed my mind.'

We did not stay long despite the Newbury Fruits looking so tempting, especially the raspberry ones.

Once outside in the street I said to Arabella, 'I didn't know you pretended to her that you were a Papist too?'

Arabella smiled with redoubled serenity.

'Supposing she goes over to Rome?' I went on. 'It will be our entire fault.'

'It won't matter if she does,' Arabella said, crossing the road in her usual confident manner, expecting all the cars to stop for her, which for some reason they always did, probably because she was so beautiful. 'After all, MI5 loves Roman Catholics now. They've even forgotten about them trying to blow up the Houses of Parliament in sixteen hundred and five.'

With that comforting thought my guilt about the Dragon disappeared, and we went to Baker Street for a coffee.

THE SECURITY FILMS

Arabella, for reasons of her own, had taken to calling my parents' elegant house in Kensington 'Dingley Dell'. Given the fact that it was, as I now saw it, playing a very important part in the security of the nation, this nickname seemed a little too light-hearted, but once Arabella seized on something, it stayed seized, and there was nothing to be done about it. My parents and myself now lived in Dingley Dell.

It was a bright late-spring morning – the sort of morning when London seems to be at its best, with the parks full of flowers, and gentlemen strolling in bowler hats to meet ladies wearing fine suiting, all of them going for lunch somewhere elegant and quiet. Arabella was not one of them, which was probably why she came up with a question for me.

'Any changes at Dingley Dell?' she wondered brightly.

I stared at her.

She had a way of knowing about things almost before they happened.

Perhaps she thought there might have been changes at home on account of the changes that had happened in our Section. The Dragon had not returned and my guilt about her had still not completely disappeared. Suppose she had turned to religion on account of my constantly blessing her? She had, according to Rosalie, gone off to Greece, to a place of repose and quiet, in order to recover her health and regain her peace of mind. That sounded to me suspiciously religious, and I was slightly comforted by the idea that if she were in a Greek convent, the religion there would be Greek Orthodox and not Roman Catholicism so I could, in a way, allow myself to feel less guilty.

'Yes, there are some changes, as a matter of fact,' I admitted, as we toyed once again with a teacake in the canteen. 'We now have lodgers in the spare bedrooms, not just guests.'

Arabella looked up from her teacake. It took a great deal to make her look up from it, especially if she happened to be partitioning it into the usual tiny portions.

'Lodgers rather than guests?' she repeated. 'Now that *is* a change.'

I could only agree by nodding because my teacake was not neatly partitioned but sliced down the middle and being scoffed in a way that I knew Arabella tried not to find off-putting – but then a great deal of what I did was upsetting to Arabella, which meant that being completely different we were quite able to be friends, whereas had I been serene and beautiful, or had she been a bit of an unmade bed, we could never have been close.

Arabella stared past me. I knew that in her own mind she was preparing to take over the Director General's job and run MI5 and, if needed, MI6, so any significant changes at Dingley Dell must be a serious matter.

'There must be a new campaign being mounted or else why would your father suddenly decide to put up with lodgers? He must be planning infiltration of some new hotbed of communism.'

I agreed although inwardly I was still bemused by the intensity of the pursuit of communism since so many of the documents I typed seemed to be full of suspicion rather than fact, but I had come to the conclusion that this was what the defence of our country must be about: deep suspicion. My mother maintained it was due to the last war when even nuns – well, especially nuns apparently – were regarded as potential spies, and people in railway carriages watched them closely to see if the black-clad women had unnaturally hairy ankles, or bosoms that kept flattening under their arms – or, in the case of suspicious men, wigs that came off with their hats when they greeted a lady, which apparently had happened once at Haywards Heath station, resulting in the immediate arrest of a person who turned out to be a very important Nazi spy. Of course they got everything they wanted out of him in the usual British way: by being nice to him and giving him Scotch whisky, which the Germans apparently loved. After that they sent him back to Sussex where they let him dig people's gardens, which he very much enjoyed, ending up marrying one of the local girls and becoming a pillar of the community.

But none of this was helping Arabella get closer to the reason why life at Dingley Dell was changing.

'Let me know the moment one of the new lodgers moves in, won't you?' she urged. 'It will be easier to work out the new thinking once we know what sort of person they are recruiting.'

I nodded and it was not long after I returned there that I realised my mother was in a state of some excitement. The first of the new lodgers had arrived, and had turned out to be a quite famous actor.

'You must remember him, Lottie. We saw him in *The Tempest*.'

My mother was theatre mad, as a result of which I was hardly out of my pram before I had seen at least two *Hamlets* and *As You Like It* and *A Midsummer Night's Dream*, not to mention *The Tempest* and *Much Ado About Nothing*. The only trouble was I couldn't remember *The Tempest* as I had drunk too much cough mixture in order not to disturb everyone around us, and had fallen sound asleep for most of the play.

'Don't tell him that,' my mother warned when I reminded her. 'Actors don't like not to be remembered.'

This was only too understandable. I myself liked to think that people would remember me, but I was unhappily aware that if they did it would not be because I had been brilliant in a Shakespeare play, but because I had done something to annoy them.

Drinks before dinner that night were interesting. Now I knew that Arabella was convinced there was a new campaign being planned, I stood about saying nothing except 'how do you do' and making the kind of sounds that female persons were meant to make in front of male persons, the kind of *marvellous, marvellous* sounds that I had observed older women making and that rendered the opposite sex terribly happy. Once we were at dinner I also used the head resting on hand approach during coffee. This worked a treat, and since it was neither a formal dinner, nor a 'bogeys only' one, the result was good. I knew it was good because I heard the soon-to-be-well-known actor telling my mother that he found me 'delightful'.

I went to bed still feeling delightful and thinking that, all in all, I would have a great deal to tell Arabella in the morning.

The next day, before I could report back, found me in the Section and my new boss, who was to my mind almost as delightful as I was, calling me in to take dictation.

He spoke so slowly that I found myself half asleep and looking back on my days with the Dragon as somewhat halcyon. At least we'd whizzed through the work whereas now, with Commander Steerforth dictating, everything seemed to happen in slow motion.

This morning, however, I noticed that he had speeded up a little, because the content of the memo I was taking down was, like the fall of the rupee, somewhat sensational. It seemed that twenty-eight security films bound for Africa had gone missing. It was particularly important that they should be found as they were full of the kind of details that were meant to help Africa, but not Russia.

I was terribly glad it was not I who had lost the twenty-eight films, but the luckless girl from Basingstoke who, happily for her, had left to marry a naval officer and gone to live in Malta, which as far as I could gather everyone who married naval officers seemed to do, including the Queen.

Commander Steerforth looked at me in gentle bewilderment.

'What can she have done with them?'

I thought for a minute.

'Perhaps she left them on a bus?'

He seemed hardly to have heard.

'It's not as if she has lost two or even three, she has lost twenty-eight.'

'Could she have perhaps sent them on to Africa and they have lost them?'

My boss shook his head.

'There will be questions asked about this,' he said gloomily. 'And I mean right up there.' He pointed at the ceiling, and we both knew what he meant: not God or heaven. He was pointing at a place where the Director General might suddenly be wondering about those twenty-eight missing security films.

'Would you like a jam doughnut?' I asked him suddenly. 'They're fresh in at the canteen.'

He looked at me; it was obvious he was sunk in gloom.

'Do you know, I would,' he said in a broken voice.

I went back to his office with a cup of tea and a jam doughnut, and that seemed to cheer him.

'What sort of security films are they?' I asked as he coped with the jam doughnut. 'I mean, what are they about?'

'Well,' he said thickly, through the doughnut, 'as I remember it they are to do with training. They show people how to do things in the correct manner, the British way, because we do have a way of doing things, and it's usually correct. At any rate, they show, again, as I remember it, how to dismantle a bomb safely – not that there is such a thing as a safe way, not really. Then, I think, taking the pin out of a grenade also with regards to safety — not that the English method can always be counted on if the grenades come from China, and — what else? Oh, yes. What to do if you tread on a bomb, but that too is a bit difficult because, as you can imagine, first aid is a bit of a waste of time if that happens.'

We looked at each other and I knew the same thought was occurring to both of us. The security films, all twenty-eight of them, sounded a bit, well — to put it mildly, a bit sort of useless really.

'Who made these films, Commander?' I asked.

'The MI5 film unit, I believe, or at least the one that we use. Most of the film people used to be part of ENSA — you know, doing comedy sketches for the Army, to keep up their spirits, and the Navy too, but less so on account of sea sickness. We had far fewer entertainers than the other services — the odd crooner, but nothing more really.'

I frowned and tried to imagine what Arabella might say. I finally arrived at: 'Perhaps it's not such a bad thing if these security films have got themselves lost?'

'How do you mean?'

'Well, from what you said, they sound a bit *de trop.*'

He stared at me and it was obvious from his expression that he did not understand French.

'I mean maybe they're not going to be much use to Africans anyway? Especially if they're lost.'

He nodded slowly.

'I think you have a point. So maybe, you're thinking, we should advise the relevant department to remove them from top-security status as being unsuitable, out of date, and not pertinent? Therefore they will no longer be sensitive material?'

That seemed the best idea to me, which was probably why I nodded my head slowly, and he did too.

'Good thinking, Lottie,' he said. 'That's the kind of thinking that won us the war.'

I returned to the Section feeling I had really come on. I had done my bit to keep the Great in Britain. Arabella was waiting to take me to lunch, not to Fenwick's, where we might be overheard, but to a bench in Green Park where we ate sandwiches.

'So what is the new lodger like?' she asked.

I stared ahead of me, knowing that she would really enjoy what I had to tell her.

'He's an actor,' I said. 'Not exactly a famous actor — more a sort of well-known one. Quite handsome actually, and charming, and going to stay at Dingley Dell for a few weeks, if not months. Of course my mother is thrilled. She really does love actors, because they make her laugh, and she doesn't have to take the ladies out to powder their noses after dinner if there's an actor there. She says that's because actors "come off it", which is nice for her because she likes people who do that. I mean,

74

some of the bogeys she knows are definitely on the stuffy side of things.'

But Arabella wasn't listening to my explanation. She was sitting cross-legged on the bench, like a fakir on a bed of nails, but not feeling anything. This was Arabella in deep, deep thought.

'Now, we have here a definite development in the thinking of MI5,' she announced. 'If Dingley Dell is going to be the base for actors who are lodging, the thinking must be that entertainments are being used as a powerful tool to convert decent people into rabid communists. They must be afraid of propaganda, of minds being subtly turned by plays and films. After all, some people I know have parents who have never allowed them to go to the cinema or the theatre, in case their minds become diseased by sex. Yes, that's it, Lottie – there are doubts abroad. They are afraid that instead of watching *Passport to Pimlico*, honest folk will start to become fascinated by films such as *I Was a Slave to Capitalism* and other X-rated filth.'

I looked at her. She was beginning to make me feel as if I was playing Watson to her Sherlock Homes, and I said as much, but Arabella was not in the least interested, too fascinated by her theories of infiltration by communists into film, and even television, although no one admitted to watching it.

'What sort of type is this actor?'

I considered for a moment.

'Very nice, charming, I told you – oh, and a Roman Catholic.'

This pleased Arabella no end.

'Well, there you are. You see, that is the thinking now: only Roman Catholicism can beat world communism on account of the Papists having so many babies. All victories depend on numbers; one of my mother's lovers told me that. You just need more people in your army than in the other army, and if you have – you win.'

It was time to go back to our Section. We walked on towards the building and once we had shown our passes, and were back up in the Section, I said to her, 'Oh, I forgot to tell you. Poor Commander Steerforth ...' I lowered my voice. 'He found out that somehow, before she left, Laetitia lost twenty-eight security films that were bound for Africa and they just can't be found. Not that they sound much good, quite frankly, but even so, they were Top Secret.'

Arabella looked vague, and I knew that was because she was still thinking about subversion through film and television.

'What did you say?'

'I said, before she left to get married, Laetitia lost twenty-eight security films.'

This time Arabella heard me. She looked at me across her typewriter and shook her head.

'She didn't lose them,' she said. 'She never lost them. She chucked them down the lift shaft. She thought they were stupid.'

I stared at her. If this was true then Commander Steerforth was out of the woods. No one in MI5 would dream of looking for security films down the lift shaft. It was bad enough getting into the lift.

'Well, that's all right,' I said happily. 'As long as they're down the lift shaft, no harm done.'

To which Arabella readily agreed.

HEARTS OF OAK

Pretty soon after MI5 had taken the decision to infiltrate show business everything started to change at Dingley Dell.

I felt mildly excited by the arrival of the first actor, and since I had feigned his religion before the Dragon so often, I felt I might be in tune with him – not that we met often. We wouldn't since I left early in the morning for MI5 and he slept in after his performance in the West End. He was appearing in an American musical comedy, actually one of my father's current favourites. Sometimes the thought did occur to me that my father might have recruited him so he could get to see the show as many times as he wished. My mother said he had seen it seven times already.

'And now he's asked the lodger to Sunday lunch, I don't suppose we will hear the end of it,' she moaned. 'You know your father and musicals. He can never get enough of them, and the worst of it is he will hum the tunes all the way home in the taxi. Heaven only knows what will happen now he has a musical-comedy star resident in the house: it will be all hell to pay. Why he couldn't have recruited some nice actor from, say, that production of *King Lear* at Stratford-upon-Avon, I don't know.'

'Probably because there are no really good tunes in *King Lear*.'

'Don't be facetious, Lottie. Just go downstairs and find out what Mrs Graham is doing to the Sunday roast and tell her not to.'

My mother closed her eyes in genuine anguish.

'Oh, lord, listen to that. They've started singing, and after only one gin and tonic. Whatever next?'

She turned back into the drawing room with the expression of someone who was about to be tortured.

I must say, I couldn't blame her. My father was not naturally musical – he just loved musicals – and unfortunately his singing was more of a dog's howl than a tuneful tenor, as I observed when I went back into the drawing room. Dear Melville Ashcombe did not seem to mind at all – or, if he did, was polite enough not to show it, happily playing and singing numbers from his show, while my mother sat staring ahead of her with a fixed smile.

Actually it was rather a jolly scene and one to which I soon found myself looking forward. It made such a change at Dingley Dell to hear the piano and singing rather than the low mutterings of my father's spooks. Mrs Graham, in the basement busy overcooking the beef, was cheered by it too.

'Nice to see your father relaxing for once,' she said, several times, before turning up the oven.

He did seem to have changed a great deal since Melville's arrival. It wasn't just the singing and humming of show numbers around the house; the fact was, whether he liked it or not, he had to act differently around actors.

'It's shaking him up a bit, this new push into theatre and film,' my mother had muttered, once or twice. 'He was always a bit of a stickler, as I think perhaps you know.'

On our first Sunday lunch with Melville I was reminded of this. Our actor friend, all geniality and good humour, had finished his lunch very quickly, in fact rather more quickly than the rest of us.

'It's all that singing and dancing you've been doing,' Mrs Graham told him, as she hurried in to serve him again. 'It must turn your insides into a crater afterwards. Starving is what you must be.'

Well, the second helping was all right, until Melville looked around for some gravy. Naturally my father passed it to him.

Melville beamed.

'Thank you, Heart of Oak,' he said.

The whole table stared at him, even Arabella who had been invited to even out the numbers.

'What was that you said? I didn't quite catch it.'

Melville managed to beam while attacking two roast potatoes and half a cow in one go.

Arabella looked across at me. She might be new to Dingley Dell but even so she realised at once from the tone that was being used – as well as my father asking a question twice – that something was up. It all signalled that he was on high alert.

Melville was oblivious. He just carried on beaming, and once the roast potatoes had been disposed of, obligingly repeated what he had just said.

'I said "thank you".'

'No, the other bit.'

'I just said – ah, yes – I just said, "Thank you, Heart of Oak."'

My father stared at him. He had a way of staring that would make any wild beast in the jungle instantly turn tail and run.

Not Melville, who just nodded happily, while his gaze remained steady, and his eyes reflected nothing but good humour.

This made my father stare harder in a way that might have disconcerted someone else. He was more used to people calling him 'sir'. 'Heart of Oak' was not at all what he was used to. But for once his hard stare fell flat. Both Arabella and I could see that. Well, it would do, because actors love people staring at them. In fact, they get quite upset if people *don't* stare at them. So my father's reproving look was a waste of time. It might work on normal spooks but not on actor-spooks.

'They're very different, actors, you know,' my father stated, thoughtfully, a few days later. 'They're not conventional, but they're very loyal and warm-hearted. I have a feeling they will be a great asset to the Office, even if they do have some funny expressions they come out with.'

Since I was working at MI5 I couldn't help being curious about what possible use someone like Melville Ashcombe would be to them.

'They will be able to tell us what is in the pipeline, what is being planned. We will find out what kind of communist-based propaganda is going to be pushed at the general public – and, more than that, we will know who is doing it. This is most important for maintaining moral standards. A country can lose its way overnight after seeing the wrong play or film. We learned that from the war. The film about Nelson, with Laurence Olivier and Vivien Leigh – it did the world of good. And the Hollywood film with that red-haired actress – not Rita Hayworth, the other one – well, it did more to bring America into the war than any of Churchill's speeches, and we all know it. Powerful stuff, film, very powerful stuff – and don't let anyone go telling you any different.'

But of course Melville was not the only actor being adopted as a lodger at Dingley Dell. There was another one in the offing, and like all would-be stars he made a delayed entrance, his tour of England in a new play taking up all his time.

*

Meanwhile at MI5, or rather in my Section, Commander Steerforth had recovered from the loss of the security films, to such an extent that now he seemed quite light-hearted and not at all interested in anything except the cakes I brought him from the canteen.

'You know, you really are the best cake-chooser,' he would say happily, and having scoffed a plateful, would sigh and look at me sadly. 'I suppose we ought to do some work.' He looked vague. 'Not that there is much to do now after the loss of the *films*.' He whispered the last word. 'The thing about that is,' he went on, 'this desk was meant to be dealing with the reaction from the other end. You know ...' He spelled out the word 'Africa' while at the same time writing it in the air. 'On receiving the *ahems*, our job was to instruct and see the whole thing through via memos and so on, but there is none of that now, due to the *ahems* never having arrived. Or, indeed, as we now surmise, never having gone.'

I was dying to tell him about the very famous star who was coming to stay with us for a few months, and about

Melville Ashcombe calling my father 'Heart of Oak' and playing the piano and singing with him, because I knew my boss would like that kind of thing, being naval and used to all the goings on below decks.

'You like films, don't you, Commander Steerforth?' I asked in order to cheer him up.

'Yes, I do, very much so – particularly with Vivien Leigh in them. I would go and see anything she was in, anything at all. And I like some of the male leads too. The actors you posted up on the section cabinets, I like their films very much, but not as much as I like Vivien Leigh's.'

'And you like the theatre too, don't you?'

'Oh, yes, I would see anything Henry Flanagan is in, for instance. He is such a fine actor. I hear he has just been touring a new play with Dame Lily Farjeon. That should be a winner, Henry Flanagan and Dame Lily – she is still a stunner. The two of them will make sparks fly, I should think. Mind you, they will need the play. The play's the thing, as we both know.'

This was too much of a test of my ability to keep my mouth shut. Any minute now I knew I would be tempted to tell him that Henry Flanagan was coming to live with us, that he was going to become an actor-spook, maybe even working in tandem with Melville Ashcombe. Sometimes I imagined them together, a darkly dressed duo darting into doorways as they saw a well-known Trotskyist they were following coming out of a coffee bar.

But tempted though I was to blurt out my Henry Flanagan news to Commander Steerforth, I knew to do so would mean that he was 'blown', and might not be able to work for my father any more. This was another golden rule that could never be broken. No spook could tell a fellow that he was a spook. He had to keep his spookiness to himself. No one had yet even told Melville Ashcombe that Henry Flanagan was coming to lodge with us, and neither of them would know of each other's role in the fight against communism. If I told Commander Steerforth my actor-spook news, I would never know the excitement of having the famous Henry Flanagan stay in the room next to mine. No person in the Section should ever talk to a colleague about their work, which was why Arabella's following the love life of a well-known lady on the intercept phones was such a daring thing to do – but then, Arabella *was* daring, and all the more so because she did not know it.

'I hope Mrs Graham can cope with two actors, not just one,' my mother said, looking worried, on the day of the expected arrival of Henry Flanagan. 'It is quite a burden, you know, two actors in one house, but your father assures me that Henry is quite house-trained and that it will just need a small adjustment and everything will continue on as smoothly as it always has. I only hope he is right. Not that I have heard anything contrary about Henry Flanagan.'

My mother might not have heard anything but from the moment he erupted from his taxi into Dingley Dell, the whole of Kensington must have heard him. He did not shout, he did not raise his voice, he just boomed – effortlessly.

'My dear lady,' he said, brushing Mrs Graham's white cotton cleaning glove with his lips. 'What a perfect delight to come and stay at your enchanting villa.'

At first Mrs Graham looked uncertain and then a little indignant, as if being mistaken for my mother was a vague insult.

'I think you had better speak to Madam, sir,' she said, quickly rubbing the back of her cleaning glove with a duster as if Henry Flanagan had been wearing lipstick and left a mark. 'Madam is in the drawing room, writing letters.'

'How very Sheridan,' Henry said, breathing in happily. 'Or do I mean how very Noël Coward? No, Sheridan, I would say. Yes, definitely Sheridan.'

Since Commander Steerforth had advised me to stay at home due to his office being painted, I was hanging about the hall pretending to be doing nothing.

The sight of Henry Flanagan was almost as impressive in its way as the sound of him. He was hugely tall, and wore the sort of clothes that I would soon grow to recognise as actor-laddie clothes. They had a hint of the olden days about them – in his case a three-piece suit, very respectable, but the shirt not closed at the collar with a tie but with a silk scarf in a bow, the whole covered with a large cape, which hung from a metal clasp. Melville's appearance always reassured, his whole look very much that of the gentleman actor. Until he said things like 'Heart of Oak', or waved his handkerchief about in the air when greeting someone, you would never really be able to distinguish him from any other member of the Garrick Club. Henry Flanagan's appearance, on the other hand, just bellowed 'actor-laddie'.

'My dear lady.' This time he was addressing not Mrs Graham, but my mother, and perhaps put off by Mrs Graham's cleaning glove, he did not kiss my mother's hand but kissed his fingers to her.

'Ah, Mr Flanagan. You have arrived safely fresh from your tour, I see,' my mother observed. 'You came by train?'

'I flew, dear lady, on the wings of hope as all we actors must, I think. And please, call me Hal, as in Prince.'

'Very well, Hal,' my mother agreed, in the tone of someone who felt she had been forced to cross some unseen boundary she might not otherwise have breached. 'Shall we ask Mrs Graham to show you to your room?'

'I can show him,' I volunteered.

'And who is this pretty young person hovering here?'

'Oh, that – that's our daughter, Lottie.'

My mother looked uneasy as if I might be about to say the wrong thing, as if I might not be able to handle this huge presence in our house.

'What a pleasure, young lady. Hal Flanagan at your feet with the rest of London, I am sure.'

I tried to smile and failed because I was already in love with Hal Flanagan – not in the conventional sense but the unconventional. He was everything I always hoped a star actor might be. He was tall, immensely good-looking and well muscled, filling out his suiting and his cloak in a way that suggested he needed only a sword to flourish. Added to which he had a great presence, absolutely dominating the drawing room, which was not small. He was just what an actor should be. He did not disappoint.

My mother called Mrs Graham, who arrived looking wary, and without gloves.

'I do love a maid,' Hal murmured to me, his eyes full of appreciation of Mrs Graham's neat appearance. 'Especially when they wear pretty aprons like that.'

'Don't call Mrs Graham a maid,' I warned him. 'She wouldn't like that, really she wouldn't. She is a daily housekeeper.'

'She has won me already,' he said happily. 'So correct, so starchy, it gets the heart quickening.'

'She is married,' I told him as I led the way up the stairs. 'Mr Graham helps here too.'

'She can play Mrs Hudson to my Sherlock Holmes any day,' Hal boomed before stopping in his tracks on seeing someone coming down the stairs towards him.

'It is bad luck to pass on the stairs, because in the old days it meant you crossed swords and that led to duels,' said Melville, standing aside for us to continue past him.

Hal too stopped, but the expression on his face changed, as did that on Melville's.

'Hal! Oh, God, Hal,' Melville said in a strangled tone. 'What are *you* doing here?'

'Good God, Melville!' said Hal. 'I could ask you the same question. I haven't seen you since — when was it last — Crewe station?'

'It's always Crewe Station,' Melville said in a suddenly bitter tone. 'Always.'

'But before that it was Benningham Rep, wasn't it?'

'I am afraid it was.'

They stared at each other, remembering.

'Which room are you in?'

'I have yet to discover, my dear Melville. All is yet to be revealed to me by this pretty young lady.'

'He is in the room next to mine,' I said, trying not to sound thrilled.

Melville nodded briefly before continuing downstairs.

'At least we are not on the same floor, Hal, that at least is a blessing.'

Hal stood still and a glint came into his eye as he watched Melville progressing down the wide staircase to the hall.

'No, I am on the floor above you, I understand. Higher up the billing, Melville. Higher up the billing.'

I don't suppose my father had ever imagined that Melville and Hal would have known each other in any particular way, and of course being of an essentially benign nature he would have been amazed to think that they were not happy in each other's company. He would assume that all actors would like all other actors, rather like people in a regiment who had to get along together or else they couldn't go about their business of defending the realm.

'Your father is a very easy-going man – that is why he makes such a deadly enemy,' my mother often said to me now I was working at MI5. 'The communists have made an enemy of him by the way they behaved in Berlin after the war, not to mention Stalin before the war ... and of course Trotsky was always such a pest.' She looked vague. 'So many of these left-wing actor types, they believe it all. They really believe everyone is born equal. As Melville said only yesterday, you would honestly have thought a few days' rehearsal would have put any idea of equality to bed for good and all.'

At that point I was happily unaware of how deep the feelings of antipathy ran between Melville and Hal, and perhaps they themselves were so shocked to discover they were sharing the same house that they were careful to avoid each other's company, which given Melville's West End commitments and Hal's daytime rehearsals was not difficult.

Obviously, having visited the house quite often now, Arabella knew not just about Melville, but about Hal, although she did not know for sure that my father had actually recruited them, but speculated about them being part of a grand MI5 plan.

I kept to the cover already agreed between my father and myself, which was that my mother had decided to take in lodgers to help cover the cost of employing the Grahams. In fact, Arabella seemed more than happy to go along with this story as her own mother had lodgers although, from the sounds of them, not quite the same type as ours.

So I was quite able to talk to Arabella about the lodgers, and she was all too eager to hear about them.

Hal being in the next-door room was a real excitement to me, because he rehearsed his lines very, very loudly. It kept me awake.

'*Poor men remain poor, rich men become richer*' was one line I would never forget; another was, '*Walk on, woman, walk on, the hill looks never so steep as when you stop*'.

Hal rehearsing his lines to himself like that went on keeping me awake until late at night, but since

Commander Steerforth had little or no work for me – and this despite the office having been repainted and both of us spending a great deal of time rearranging the cabinets and the shelves several times – my being a bit tired at work did not seem to matter.

However such was not the case with Melville. He came back late at night and he too was kept awake by the booming of Hal's lines, and this would not do. He took to banging on the ceiling above his bed and shouting 'Do belt up, Hal!', which seemed only to make him boom louder. Happily my parents' suite was on the other side of the house and they were left serenely undisturbed, until daytime dawned, and the telephone started ringing, in a way that upset my mother.

'It is all very well your father going about saying what an asset Melville and Hal are going to be to his work, he does not have to deal with their agents ringing up all the time. I mean, yesterday Hal's agent became a bit offhand because Mrs Graham did not immediately pass on a message about Denham Studios. She can't be expected to act as his secretary, really she can't.' My mother shook her head. 'I only hope your father is pursuing the right line in using actors for his work. For myself, I think they're going to prove to be a marsh light, just leading him on, and he will end up in the swamp.'

Before the threat of the marsh light leading the occupants of Dingley Dell on towards their squelchy doom could manifest itself, Sunday lunch came round again, as it is prone to do.

As before, Sunday lunch opened with Melville, having been to church, seating himself at the piano and beginning to play and sing. My father leaned on it and happily joined in, all the while sounding more and more like a howling wolf.

My mother sipped her sherry and read a book, wearing the expression of someone in a public library, who has to put up with noise but is hard put to look as if she is enjoying it.

Melville and my father were in the middle of a particularly rousing drinking song, I happened to know it was one of my father's favourites, when the door opened and Hal walked in. Naturally the happy pair around the piano did not stop singing, or – in my father's case – howling, but merely carried on enjoying themselves.

'Do help yourself to a drink, Hal,' my mother called to him above the uproar. She indicated the Dingley Dell drinks cupboard whose doors, according to Mrs Graham, had been left open since the start of the last war.

'Your father is the most generous man,' she would say proudly. 'Doesn't matter who passes by, if they want a drink they can take one, help themselves to whatever they want. And the result is, of course, no one does.'

Hal stood and surveyed the drinks, and then taking a large Waterford tumbler he poured himself a whisky so large that my mother put her sherry glass down and stood up and sat down again as if she had just heard the low moan of a doodlebug.

'Gracious,' she said, as Hal drank it down in what seemed like one. 'You are thirsty.' And then she added, over-brightly, as she sat down again: 'How are rehearsals going, Hal?'

'Dreadfully,' he boomed, before walking over to the piano and starting to join in the drinking song.

Of course my father loved it. I could see that, singing with his two actor-spooks around the piano, he could imagine he was not just at a musical, he was in one.

Before we went in to lunch he insisted on Melville singing the best number from his show. This did not go down well with Hal, who went and stood by the window, making sure that my mother and I could see him as he quite obviously practised his lines despite the intrusion of the piano and the singing.

Over lunch the small matter of their old days in repertory together came up. I say, a small matter. That is not right. It was quite obviously of huge concern to them, and the stories they told about it were hilari-ous: of the sea washing into dressing rooms, of leading ladies who pulled each other's wigs off, of leading men whose tights ripped as they duelled, of scenery that went missing so that looking for 'yonder window' was impossible since yonder window had failed to appear.

In fact, it seemed that scenery had a habit of disappearing never to be seen again, or else appearing in the wrong act, so hapless actors found themselves arriving out of fireplaces to play what should have been moving and dramatic scenes, only to be greeted with howls of laughter. One star actor was in the habit of pasting his lines on to prop trees, only to find them changed around by the stage hands because they hadn't been paid.

'I fail to see how this has anything to do with the fight against communism,' I heard my mother grumbling to my father the following day, but since we were all invited to Hal's first night, she was prepared to be mollified.

'Break a leg, Hal,' Melville called as his rival left that morning for the theatre.

'I wish I could, dear boy, I wish I could. Dame Lil is such a pill, I wish I could break both my legs.'

A West End opening night was always inclined to be glamorous, and even more so if it starred a famous name. Dame Lily Farjeon was extremely famous, Henry Flanagan a little less so. Nevertheless their joint names lit up Shaftesbury Avenue, and seeing them certainly made an impression on my parents and myself.

'Hal said Dame Lily is so convinced her lettering's smaller than his,' my mother informed us, nodding to the sign, 'she sent someone up a ladder yesterday with a tape measure.'

'Looks all right to me,' my father said, peering at it. 'But I gather Dame Lily is a bit of a stickler.'

'That's not what they called women like her when I was growing up,' my mother announced, walking ahead of us into the theatre.

I had quite forgotten that, what with Hal rehearsing next-door far into the night, I knew most of his lines.

My mother did not have that luxury, but she did have an opinion about what she was seeing, and shortly into the first act, what with Dame Lily in rags and one thing and another, suddenly opined: 'Of course, this is all nonsense, you realise, don't you?'

Despite knowing parts of it so well, I could not but agree.

'And, Lottie, do stop mouthing all the lines. It's bad enough having to hear them spoken.'

Of course I stopped, but not just to please my mother. I stopped because I realised that Hal had forgotten a sizeable chunk, but only I, and possibly Dame Lily Farjeon, knew it. Certainly he seemed completely out of sorts during the whole first act, so much so that some of the audience started to walk out in that really loud way people will do when they think their money has been wasted.

'Our lodger seems to be a bit ill at ease,' my father said over interval drinks.

My mother stared at the programme.

'Awful to have to play such a part – I mean, Common Man. Who in their right mind would want a part like that? And why is Dame Lily always walking up a hill in those dreadful clothes? Surely Common Man should stop standing around and help her with whatever she has on her back?'

My mother flicked through the rest of the programme as if trying to find out if there were more actors about to come on in the second act, only to find advertisements for hand cream and Greek restaurants.

'I gather the thing on her back is a metaphor,' my father offered, looking around for an ashtray.

'Well, whatever it is, it is obviously as heavy as the play. Really, you would have thought that Dame Lily could have found something else to be in.'

'Hal told me she wanted a change of direction, something to get her teeth into. She is fed up with teacups and drawing-room windows and plays that require her to look beautiful.'

'She must be pleased then, she looks dreadful. Actresses should stick to what they do best. Who dragged this play up for her?'

'It came from Berlin.'

'As if we haven't had enough trouble out of there without them sending us their awful plays! And why is Hal coughing so much? Shouldn't he take something for that?'

'That's in the play, he is a diseased capitalist,' I said, full of self-importance.

My mother ignored this. 'I thought you said this play was sure to make waves,' she went on, looking accusingly at my father, as if it was his fault that our evening was proving to be so boring. 'From what we have seen so far, it will have a hard job making a ripple.'

My father nodded. I could tell that he appreciated my mother's point, but I could see something else too. It was the look that his eyes always took on when he knew he had an ace up his sleeve.

The second act remained as turgid as the first with Common Man taunting Poor Woman, and finally taking her burden from her back, which for some reason made her not grateful but very upset. Dame Lily cried very well – well, actually she didn't cry, she screamed that she wanted her burden returned to her, but to no avail. Common Man went off with it and became a Rich Capitalist, and so Poor Woman was left to trudge uphill once more, to the accompaniment of some terrible music.

The applause at the end was tepid – what my mother called 'bathwater after the war'; and although we went backstage afterwards, we knew we should only stay for a minute or two because Hal said he was intent on getting drunk, and my mother said we really shouldn't stand in his way.

The notices the next morning were understandably terrible. What a waste of talents such as Dame Lily Farjeon and Henry Flanagan. One critic even wondered whether, since so much had gone wrong, the play would go down in the annals of Famous Flop First Nights.

Hal being in a flop was sad for him, but at least it meant I could enjoy a good night's sleep. Of course once the play closed, which it did within a matter of days, Hal did nothing but sleep, because there was nothing else for him to do. This did not go down well with Mrs Graham.

'I'm not used to making beds at four in the afternoon,' she grumbled. 'It's just not good housekeeping.'

I could see her point, but I felt sorry for Hal. Even if he had always known he was touring in a turkey, as he had called it, it did not mean that the blow was easier to bear.

Melville was wise about it.

'He had to do it on account of Dame Lily. She gets them in, but from what I have heard, not even she could fill in that piece,' he said, before letting his hands take charge and playing some commanding opening chords. In fact so commanding were they that, on hearing them, Mrs Graham rushed into the drawing room and announced that the curtain was rising on Sunday lunch in fifteen minutes.

And indeed it was. Over lunch we all managed to cheer Hal up, and he, resuming his role as actor-laddie, rose to the occasion.

'My agent told me that everyone is blaming Dame Lily,' he boomed, 'for choosing such a load of left-wing tripe. He said it should have closed after Brighton.'

At that of course I pricked up my ears. I might not have worked at MI5 for very long but I knew my duty and, at the words 'left-wing tripe', alarm bells rang in my head.

'So would *you* say Hal's play was very left-wing?' I asked my father, all innocence, a few days later.

'Oh, yes,' he said, imperturbably. 'And it's never a good idea really to put any kind of politics into a play. Just write the story and the politics will take care of themselves.' He paused. 'Of course, poor Hal is feeling it a bit now, but he's got a good part coming up at Denham Studios with a friend of mine. A film producer, nice chap – drinks a bit, but then don't they all? He's come to the rescue and offered something to Hal that will be just the ticket.'

I was too curious to leave it at that, and besides it was a fact that when my father was in a good mood, that was the time to take ruthless advantage of him.

At the moment he was staring out of the drawing-room window at nothing in particular, which was a habit of his when he was feeling at ease with the world.

'Well, that is good,' I agreed, and although I could see he was still in a beneficent mood, I decided not to push my luck, and turned to go. Perhaps he sensed that I would have liked to know more because he stopped me by continuing to speak.

'This other chap, a director, likes to be helpful to the Office. As a matter of fact, it was he who managed to talk Dame Lily Farjeon into doing the play ... told her it was going to be the challenge of her career, change her category, take London by storm. She fell for it, of course.'

'Yes, she did, poor lady,' I agreed.

My father was now moving towards his drink cupboard, preparing for what he always called 'an opener'. He poured himself a Scotch and gave me a glass of wine, which he kept especially for Arabella and myself, 'young wine for the young' he called it.

'Of course, that is not the end of the story,' he went on, after he had settled back in his favourite chair, and once more that familiar look came into his eyes. I stared at him, knowing he was about to take the ace from his sleeve.

After a long pause, during which he lit a cigarette and exhaled appreciatively, he continued.

'Once our contact had talked her into doing the part, his theatre management was able to raise the money to back the play; because of her name, the fact that, like Vivien Leigh, dear Dame Lily always fills, and because of the nature of the play – the Trotskyists put rather a large amount of party funds in it, and now of course they've lost the lot.' He ran a finger across his upper lip where I imagined he might once have sported a moustache. 'Bit of a pity for them, of course, but there you are. All's fair, as they say.'

Now I knew just why I had seen that particular expression in my father's eyes on the play's opening night. It was almost as contented as when he was with Melville, playing and singing at the drawing-room piano – almost, but not quite.

MATER HARI

I had given up learning Latin after my first lesson, but even I knew that Mater meant Mother in Latin. For some reason I couldn't be bothered to find out from Arabella why she so often referred to her mother in that way.

'Careful where you go – new gent in Mater's life,' she said shortly after she asked me up to her mother's flat for a coffee one Saturday. She nodded towards what I realised must be the main bedroom, and we both walked quickly past and into the large kitchen, which was furnished by racks of wine and a maid in a navy blue uniform.

'We want a coffee, please, Maria Constanza,' Arabella told her.

While the maid made the coffee I looked around in some amazement for not only was the kitchen fully stocked with wine, it was also host to a great many bottles of vodka; and when the maid opened the fridge door, I saw that inside its impressive interior was stacked jars of caviar, their gleaming contents only waiting, I imagined, to be enjoyed with hot toast and butter.

'The new gent is very generous,' Arabella said, but she spoke behind a raised hand, making sure only I saw what she was saying.

I was only too happy that Maria Constanza had her back to us or she might have suspected Arabella of not trusting her. As it was she put the coffee pot down in front of us in such a way that I felt she really did not feel a great deal of affection for Arabella.

'She's a spy,' Arabella said in a low voice the moment the poor woman had left the room. 'She thinks I don't know that she is always listening in at doors and going through my mother's handbag.'

I frowned. I couldn't understand why the maid should be spying on Arabella's mother, or Mater. As far as I could gather, she was once a famous Society beauty and was still only interested in what could loosely be called her social life.

'Perhaps Maria Constanza is just nosy?' I ventured.

'I'll say she's nosy – and she makes lousy coffee,' Arabella agreed. Getting up, she threw the contents of the pot away and made some more coffee.

'I don't touch what she puts in front of me,' she said, nodding towards the closed kitchen door. 'Really I wonder that Mater does, but you can't tell her anything.'

I felt distinctly uneasy, as anyone would. It was one thing to have actor-spooks living at home, because after all my father was running them, but quite another to go into a luxurious Knightsbridge flat owned by a lady with a reputation for having very round heels, and find that the food and drink might be suspect. This was feeling the icy draught from the Cold War blowing too close for comfort.

I returned to the subject, determined to find out more, because I knew Arabella did not get flapped easily and I could see that underneath her once again serene exterior she was uneasy, and that was not like her. I thought she might be too suspicious of the maid, but even so I was glad that she had made us fresh coffee, for my grandmother always said you never knew what foreign servants were up to, until they left.

The following day I went into Commander Steerforth's office hoping against hope that he would have some work to alleviate my coffee and tea breaks. He had a couple of short memos to be typed in reply to other officers' memos, following which I sat with my shorthand notebook and pencil playing Hangman and he ruminated, something at which he was rather good.

'I forgot to ask you last week. Did you attend the unfortunate first night of Dame Lily Farjeon's play?' he finally asked after I had observed it was his coffee break and furnished him with two iced buns and a large sugary coffee.

I told him I had attended the first night, and then fell silent. I felt I knew too much about everything to do with that play to be able to add anything more than that it was now a well-established flop.

'Dame Lily has a bit of a reputation, you know,' the Commander said, lowering his voice. 'An unfortunate tendency to meddle in affairs that are really above her beautiful head.' He reached forward and placed a file in front of him. 'We have confidential reports here about her political activities, and I can only tell you that they make interesting reading. She has even signed a petition to Save the Verse Play, which is unfortunate to say the least.'

Commander Steerforth sighed.

'I do wish actresses would just keep to what they do best. It's so much better to be worshipped from over the footlights, tread the boards, become the magical beings created by Shakespeare and others, and leave all the politics to people who can't do any of those things. Lift our spirits, allow us to worship you, but keep away from political people who are determined to make our lives miserable. Vivien Leigh would never get involved above her beautiful head. She is only interested in herself and her career, and that is how it should be.'

This was as emotional as I had ever seen Commander Steerforth except when I once brought some of Mrs Graham's very special chocolate cake from home, when his eyes had filled with what looked like something very close to tears.

I felt I should try to defend Dame Lily without giving away anything too sensitive.

'I understand that she was talked into doing the play by an old friend. Apparently she only did it as a favour to him.'

'Really, is that true? In that case, no more to be said. Despite everything she obviously has a heart of gold, and in time we may even forgive her support for the Verse Play.' He closed the file again. 'There is nothing here of much interest,' he said happily. 'And if the play closed that is all that matters. She just made a silly mistake, talked into it by some left-leaning jack-the-lad. Now here is a more serious matter that has come to light.'

He reached for another file.

I stared at him. The name on the file was unmistakable.

'Obviously we never discuss each other's information, but I think you know the person involved here.'

I nodded.

'You have been to the premises where some of the events detailed in here have taken place.'

I had never felt more uneasy. This was worse than my father breaking into a friend's house. Commander Steerforth was pointing to an address that we both knew was that of my best friend's mother's flat.

'I was there on Saturday,' I admitted.

'Saturday? Did you notice anything in particular?'

'How do you mean?' I asked, cautiously.

'Anything unusual?'

'There was a foreign maid.'

'Did she speak Russian?'

'No, but there was a great deal of vodka and caviar about the place,' I burst out, and immediately felt as if I had handed Arabella and her mother over to the police.

Commander Steerforth's eyes lit up to maximum iced-bun alert.

'My goodness, you have been useful.' He looked at me. 'Do you think you would like me to ask your father if you could go on active service?'

My mouth went dry. I had never been someone who liked to be active, unless you could call running after the number nine bus active. The very suggestion of any kind of team sports was enough to make me report to Matron instantly.

'I am not suitable to be active, Commander,' I said, making my voice sound suddenly reedy and weak. 'I never usually say anything, of course, but my health is not the greatest. Why, even to get in here – I can tell you now, I was convinced I would not pass a medical.'

'They don't have medicals here,' Commander Steerforth said, and then he frowned. 'Perhaps they should.' He made a note on his pristine notepad. 'I will bring that up at the next Section meeting. We really should keep an eye on our health, and that of our agents, it is only sensible. Particularly agents ... they might have anything.' He turned his attention back to me. 'So you don't think you are up to active service?'

'I am afraid not,' I sighed. 'I like the idea, of course. I want to do everything I can to help MI5 and be an asset to them. I want to defend our country against Trotskyists and people who sign petitions to Save the Verse Play, but I just don't have the stamina. My mother has always said I was born feeble.'

'You're outstanding when it comes to choosing cakes,' Commander Steerforth said, after a short pause while he obviously tried to think of something I was good at. 'Top marks. I have put that on your monthly assessment, that and the fact you take shorthand so well. My last secretary, the late Laetitia, used to fall asleep all the time.'

I sighed inwardly in relief. I had obviously passed my monthly behavioural assessment.

'That was very kind of you, Commander,' I said before returning to my Section. I thought no more about it until he called me back the following afternoon.

He looked excited, as if a very brilliant thought had arrived at last.

'They've got a spiffing Victoria sponge fresh in,' I told him. 'Really good and squishy, lots of jam. One of the waitresses' mother has taken up making them.'

I knew at once that a hugely important notion must have come to him when he failed to take me up on the Victoria sponge.

'I have been thinking, overnight and again this morning, about you. While I appreciate you are not the type to go on active, active service, for health reasons and so on, nevertheless it seems to me that you could go on inactive service.'

I stared at him.

'How do you mean?' I asked, my voice returning to weak and reedy.

Commander Steerforth pushed his chair away from his desk so that he faced me full on, which he never usually did. It was ominous.

'You are, at this moment, uniquely positioned to be on inactive service. Nothing need change in your life, which is why it is called inactive service, but you can be of great use in the case of the lady whom the Service is now calling Mater Hari.'

I was to spy on Arabella's mother? The very idea was appalling.

'I haven't even met the lady in question, Commander, only had coffee in her flat, and seen a whole lot of vodka and caviar. That's not enough to make me an agent surely?'

'It is quite enough,' he replied robustly. 'Why, I have known people become agents just because they heard someone talking foreign on a train. Spies are made like this. Added to which,' he gave me an appreciative look, 'you are so unlike one, who on earth would take you for a spy? No one in their right mind would ever suspect you to be any more than a pretty young popsy.'

I thought for a minute. I knew he meant well, but I still didn't like the idea of being a popsy at all. It sounded like the sort of person who was always doing the Charleston on a table top, or coming out of a wine cooler in a bikini in the middle of a regimental dinner. I indicated this to Commander Steerforth, and he laughed rather too loudly.

'That is exactly what I mean,' he said. 'It is exactly why no one will suspect you – you are just what they used to call "too-too" to be suspicious.'

'Yes, but even so, I would suspect me, really I would. I would be the first person to suspect me, simply because I am not at all suspicious,' I insisted.

'Good thinking. In that case we had better make sure you do something suspicious and then no one will suspect you. Leave that to me. It might take time, but I am sure I will be able to come up with something.'

'What about the Victoria sponge?'

'What about it?'

'Shall I bring you a piece?'

'Of course, of course, and by the time you come back I will have something for you.'

Thankfully Commander Steerforth did not come up with something so quickly; even so my journey home was miserable. Although I had only a vague idea of what a cleft stick might be, I knew I must be balancing in one, and I was certainly on the horns of a dilemma.

My father was standing by the drinks cupboard. I thought he might be able to help me get out of being on inactive service, but since Hal had just come into the room and they were about to take their drinks into the garden and mutter, which men seemed to have a habit of doing, I knew this was not the time to ask him. Besides which, the whole idea was highly sensitive, seeing that it involved Russian gents lurking about luxury flats in Knightsbridge. I didn't even know whether I should tell him, and worse than that, there was always the risk that he might undertake to bungle a burglary at Mater's flat.

That night, for the first time in many months, I flung open my bedroom window and made another attempt at getting pneumonia. Unfortunately I only got cold, and ended up having to take myself off for a hot bath, during which I tried to think of some other way out of my current situation.

I did not want to spy on Arabella's mother, but neither did I want to let down Commander Steerforth, my Section, and my country. I plumped for a plan I had quite often plumped for before – I would do nothing. I would leave it to Fate and Commander Steerforth, and hope that nothing came of his bright idea.

The trouble with doing nothing, I realised the following Saturday, is that nothing very often leads to something.

To my great consternation, Commander Steerforth had come up with something for me to do, and as a result I was once more having coffee with Arabella.

'I would love to meet your mother,' I ventured – this being part of the Steerforth Notion. 'I've heard so much about her, especially how beautiful she is. She has been painted by everyone famous, hasn't she?'

Arabella nodded, but the expression in her eyes was one of deep suspicion. She was no fool, as I knew well, and once she moved off her bed of nails, she could put three and three together and come up with some amazing results.

'You can meet my mother,' she announced, after a pause, 'always providing you tell me why you really want to meet her?'

For no reason I remembered Melville telling me that Noël Coward had been in the habit of smuggling currency after the war, and that he used to say to the Customs Officers 'do hurry up, my feet are killing me, it's all the pound notes in my shoes', which apparently the Customs Officers always found hilarious, and as a result they let him through even faster.

I stared straight-faced at Arabella.

'I want to meet your mother so I can spy on her,' I said.

Arabella started to laugh.

'Of course that's why. Well, as a matter of fact, she is actually awake and Lover Boy is away, so you can certainly meet her, but don't be surprised when you do. She is quite a number is Mater.'

After a short interval we went through to the drawing room and waited. Eventually a sound was heard. It was Mater. She was singing and rather well too, I thought, although Arabella raised her eyes to heaven as if to indicate that this was just something we would have to put up with.

In Mater came, and I could see at once why so many famous painters had once begged her to sit to them. She was older now, of course, but still inexpressibly lovely. Her golden hair and blue eyes, her high cheekbones, her delicate features, were quite extraordinary.

'You're Lottie,' she announced, looking at me. 'You're exactly how I imagined you.'

This set me back. I had no idea why anyone like Mater should ever have spent any time imagining what I would be like.

'How do you do?' I greeted her. And then, in a moment of inspiration, added, 'You are even more beautiful than I imagined.'

It was creepy, but it seemed to work because she smiled and sank back against a mountain of silk cushions.

'Actually Lottie is here to spy on you,' Arabella told her, and Mater laughed.

'Spies, spies, spies – that is all people think about nowadays. Bad enough during the war when they would keep locking up nuns, poor things, but now every other person with a foreign accent has to be a spy. The whole thing is nonsense, and such a waste of public money. Half my friends are foreign, and they are always under suspicion. It is just so irksome for them.'

I was impressed that she obviously knew that her friends were being watched, and I wondered whether the Steerforth Notion was not as new to the thinking of MI5 as I'd imagined. It was really rather strange for Mater to come out with this so soon into our acquaintance.

'Fetch me a vodka, would you, Arabella?'

Most older women drank gin or sherry. I had never heard of any of my friends' mothers or my mother's friends drinking vodka. This was all too *Ninotchka* for words. And I was suddenly afraid I was being drawn into a situation that might be going to prove too much for me. The ghastly thought crossed my mind that I might even now be called upon to be on active rather than inactive service.

Arabella returned with vodka and Mater took an appreciative sip of it.

'So much that the authorities do to my friends is so obvious,' she continued. 'For instance, listening in to telephone conversations. The moment you pick up the receiver' – she reached for her impressively Hollywood-style white telephone on the table beside her – 'hear that? It clicks!' She seemed very pleased that she was being tapped. 'I mean you would think that someone would tell them we all know when that happens not to say anything that might make life difficult for our foreign friends. It is really too silly for them to be blind to how obvious they are.' She looked at us. 'I am always saying to Arabella, if only she worked somewhere interesting like MI5, instead of the boring old War Office, I would get her to tell someone higher up in the government what cracking asses they are making of themselves. You would never find the Russians being so obvious, but they have been at it, as it were, for centuries.'

Russians being 'at it' was a particularly unfortunate phrase, which was probably why Arabella left the room in search of a bitter lemon for us both, leaving me alone with Mater.

'So your father works in the War Office too. How very dull for him. Does he find it dull?'

'Oh, yes,' I lied. 'He finds it very dull, particularly now there are hardly any wars on.'

The telephone rang. Mater picked up.

'No, this is not Trigata,' she said in a resigned tone. 'No, it is no good your insisting. This is not an import–export business – it is the private residence of one who is growing increasingly irritated by your calls. We do not stock anything you would wish to acquire. Goodbye.' She picked up her drink and sipped at it for a moment.

'Really, what is happening around here when people seeking an import–export business will not leave us alone?'

I did not think too much about that interruption, at least not at that moment, until as an agent on inactive service, I reported back to Commander Steerforth the following Monday.

'Nothing happened at all, but she does know … no, all her foreign friends who are under suspicion, *they* all know … that their telephone calls are being tapped. There is a click before you hear the normal tone. It is quite obvious, apparently.'

Commander Steerforth stared at me.

'A click, did you say?'

'Yes, quite a loud one,' I said, exaggerating, full of self-importance.

He thought for a minute, and as always it felt as if I could not only hear the wheels of thought going round, I could actually see them – a bit like in a flour mill. Which might be the reason why the Commander liked cakes so much. Perhaps they slowed up the thought processes?

'I never knew that,' he said eventually. 'I never knew that there was a click. Quite a loud one, you say?'

'Well, I imagine it must be loud,' I said, backtracking quickly in case I was going to get the third degree for not being entirely accurate. 'If all these foreign friends of hers know about it.'

'Something must be done,' Commander Steerforth announced suddenly. 'Although what, I wouldn't know. The boffins who go in for this sort of thing are frightfully slow. Their brains take longer to warm up than the average person's, I always say. Tell a boffin something and they just scribble down a whole lot of numbers, and then subtract them, and then add them up again, and at the end of it you can be sure that the click on the telephones will still be as loud as it ever was. I've seen it in action, I tell you. As soon as they start saying X equals Y, best be on your guard. It's all wool-pulling.'

I nodded but my mind was on other things as I was feeling quite hungry. Arabella had discovered that the coffee bar round the corner did a mean line in Spaghetti Bolognese and I was anxious to meet her there as near to midday as possible, that being the time when you could not only get a seat, but also a reduction on the menu price.

'Well now, I don't suppose you feel you have done much, young Lottie,' Commander Steerforth was saying when I came back to earth from my pre-lunch fantasies. 'But you have. You have already done a great deal on inactive service. But I have to ask you once again, just to be on the safe side. Was there anything else you noticed that you might perhaps have forgotten to mention?'

I pulled myself back from thinking about food, which as usual was difficult for me, and in an effort to look more active, I frowned.

'The lady in question,' I said carefully, 'is very beautiful. And she drinks vodka.'

At the mention of vodka Commander Steerforth immediately looked on high alert.

'This is noteworthy,' he said. 'Did you note the label?'

As a matter of fact I had noted the name on it down when Arabella had left the room only because it was in Russian. I reached into my handbag and showed Commander Steerforth the back of my chequebook, where I had written down the name in lipstick after leaving the flat.

'I see.' Commander Steerforth nodded, his expression serious. 'This is in Russian. It must be Russian vodka. Well done! Well done indeed. You might seem to be a bit fluffy but you have the right instincts – and you know something?'

I didn't, but I did remember to look modest because I thought he might be going to compliment me.

'You can't make an agent, whether active or inactive. It has to be already in here.' He tapped his chest, lightly. 'And of course with you it is in the blood. We will trace this lipstick of yours – I mean, we will trace this make of vodka and go to the source. That will be a good start.'

'I think you should try Harrods wine department. The lady in question apparently shops nowhere else.'

'Good, good. More unravelling. Just what we need. Was there anything else you noted with your Eye Spy with My Little Eye eyes?'

'Nothing I actually saw — but there was something else, namely a telephone call from an import–export company. Apparently they keep calling her and she has to struggle to understand their foreign accents. She finds it very dull.'

'Did you note the name of this import–export company?'

I consulted the back of my chequebook again.

'Trigata,' I told him, spelling it out slowly because the lipstick was a bit smudged. 'They keep on ringing her up and she has no idea why.'

Following this, Commander Steerforth sent me to Files to find out if they had anything on a company called Trigata. They had nothing. It was disappointing, but in another way good for me because he felt his inactive agent had done so well that he let her off early for lunch, to meet Arabella and talk men over spaghetti.

Basically she had been put off them by her mother.

'Mater's attitude to the opposite sex is not what you would call everyday,' Arabella told me, but only after we had whopped up the spaghetti. 'What she feels about men could be written on the back of your chequebook.'

I immediately felt I was under suspicion. Had Arabella seen the lipstick marks? I thought not, I hoped not, I prayed that her mentioning my chequebook was just a coincidence.

'Yes, but what exactly would you write on it, if you don't mind my asking?'

'Give me your chequebook and I will show you.'

I handed it over after thanking God, who was presumably a committed anti-communist, that I had had the foresight to tear off the back and give it to Commander Steerforth to put in his safe, which he had duly done.

After I had handed her my backless chequebook, she wrote something on the last page.

What she wrote made dreadful reading.

'Is that really what your mother thinks of the opposite sex?' I asked.

Arabella, at her most sphinx-like, nodded slowly.

'Yes, that is what Mater thinks of men. She has told me so many times, and nothing will change her mind.'

'What about your father, though?'

'It was a weekend marriage, and then he went away and never came back. The war, you know. But Mater always says she had a great war, and won't hear a word against it.'

I frowned. I had heard people say this or variations of it before, mostly friends of my parents. Some even said 'I had a *wonderful war*', which always made me wonder what on earth they'd been doing to have such a wonderful time when there was a world war raging. My mother was able to explain it a little; although she would never really betray her own generation, she nevertheless gave intimations sometimes.

'The men, you know, they needed their comforts,' she would say, at her vaguest.

This was a metaphor, I knew enough to realise that, but still it led me to believe that all these women who had enjoyed a wonderful war had been rushing about making hot drinks and filling hot water bottles to comfort the men, until my mother added cryptically that of course some of the women earned themselves a bit of a reputation. So that ruled out hot water bottles and cocoa, I could see. No one ever got a bad reputation for filling a hot water bottle. No – this was obviously far more to do with the kind of thing hinted at on Bognor Beach.

'So would you say that your mother's war became a way of life?' I asked, trying to sound delicate.

'No doubt about it,' Arabella agreed. 'Coffee?'

The coffee was delicious, but it did nothing to make me feel better about Mater whom I now felt I was probably sending to be shot as a spy for drinking vodka with a funny label on it and taking unwanted calls from an import–export business.

'How do *you* feel about men?' I asked Arabella.

'I don't know any,' she said factually. 'Only the odd types who come to the flat and you wouldn't want to go near them with a toasting fork. And of course the men at the Office, but they're not really men, are they? They're all types, which is different. Army type, Navy type, civil servant type, and so on. The men I would like to meet simply don't exist.'

'Suppose you tell me what you would like in a man?'

Arabella looked at me and smiled. She had a smile that went up to her eyes, which I always find reassuring.

'Very well. First of all he would be handsome, but not in a very overt way, as in not the door flinging open and you see a stunning face looking at you. No, no – not like that at all. More an *engaging* face. Large eyes, of course, and a broad forehead, which would tell you he has brains. I would like him to be tall, because tall men are less likely to bully, but most of all he would be funny – not as in telling jokes because that's awful – just funny with a squiffy way of looking at life, you know, the way some people are.' She stared at me. 'But then no one ever meets someone like that, do they? Funny and handsome, someone who is always doing romantic things, always thinking of things that might enchant you. Such men do not exist.'

The more I thought about it, the more it seemed to me that Arabella might have a point.

'The best men are the male heroes created in fiction – by women,' she went on, pressing home her point as she saw that I was now thrown into some considerable doubt about the opposite sex.

'The Scarlet Pimpernel, Heathcliff, Rhett Butler, Mr Darcy – all created by women, and that is because they couldn't find a man they really liked, which made them sit down and create one.'

Arabella looked understandably proud of the point she had made. I felt crushed. I knew I was not a very romantic person, but the idea that the only really fascinating men were created by women saddened me.

Back at the Office I passed through the usual security checks with a smile and a joke, thinking that the afternoon promised to be a little less fraught and I would soon be back on the number nine bus and going on to a bottle party at my cousin Jamie's flat. That was what I was looking forward to, but I had not counted on Commander Steerforth whose mill-like brain was obviously now grinding busily.

'Something of great significance has come up,' he said. 'I have cross-referenced Trigata – the import–export business that you divulged to me earlier.'

I tried not to look shocked. I'd had no idea that I was capable of divulging anything. It didn't sound the sort of thing I was brought up to do.

'Yes – and you are on to something there, something of great interest to us. Well done! No one suspected Trigata until now, not even the lady who was being plagued by their calls. They are a hotbed of enemy agents.'

I looked at him, astonished.

'Trigata are also the source of the vodka and caviar. They are using this import–export lark as a cover for infiltration, and the love interest of the lady in question, a certain Sergei, is a second secretary at a certain embassy. And we all know what *they* are.'

I didn't like to say that I didn't even know what first secretaries were like.

I must have looked blank, which was not difficult for me, because Commander Steerforth tapped his desk.

'Come on, come on – secretaries at embassies are always spies. It's *de rigueur*.' He sighed in a rather happy way. 'Yes, they know ours are and we know theirs are, and the lady in question has been entertaining this particular second secretary – this Sergei – for some months now. So Trigata, thanks to you, will now have its telephone tapped.' He looked at me. 'Of course you know that the lady in question is one of us?'

'How do you mean?'

We both knew what he meant. She was a plant, but not the kind you saw at the Chelsea Flower Show.

'She started during the war in SOE. Very brave, you know, and she's sort of gone on from there. She was brilliant in the war. I cannot divulge more, but believe me the Office is very grateful to her, and the luxury she lives in is a very small price for us to pay.'

I could only feel relieved that the Commander's habit of divulging things was at an end, at least for that afternoon anyway, but even so I turned to go back to the Section with my head reeling. Arabella's mother was a beautiful and brilliant double agent, and this despite my father telling me that he knew of very few beautiful agents except in fiction. All that business of having

125

her on file – that had to be to fool anyone who might themselves be an undercover agent. I mean, the other side had to suspect that she was one of them. It was that simple – and that complicated.

I couldn't even ask Arabella if she knew what I knew. I could only assume that she didn't. So I went to my cousin Jamie's bottle party with several bottles of my father's youngest wine, and I am sorry to say the party was made all the better for my knowing there was not a spook in sight. At least that was what I thought, but of course knowing what I now knew, I also knew that I couldn't be quite sure. The truth was, whether I liked it or not, I was well and truly spooked.

THE RUNNING BUFFET

The atmosphere at Dingley Dell was calm, if a little grey around the edges. The calm was due to the routine into which the house had settled, this being one where Mrs Graham grumbled, my mother looked saintly, and Hal sat about looking morose, which did not suit him. His filming had come to an end, and although he had been flattered that he had been given a trailer for the first time, he hated filming and longed only to get back to the theatre, but theatre had not recovered from his last appearance, so no new offers were coming his way

I think my father must have felt a bit sensitive about the fact that he had manipulated Hal, not to mention Dame Lily, into doing a play that had only lasted three days, but even he could do nothing about theatre managements. When an actor was on the back burner he tended to remain isolated there, until such time as something happened to change everything – which it sometimes didn't.

Hal was on the back burner all right, and the dreadful play from Berlin had put him there. Something had to be done, not least to relieve my mother because Hal was constantly under her feet. She complained that not only did he and Melville constantly use the telephone to ring their agents, but the agents constantly rang the house, in order to take an inordinate amount of time telling either Melville or Hal that there was no work for them.

When he wasn't taking phone calls, or making phone calls, Hal would sit staring blankly at the telephone. Whenever I saw him it seemed to me that he was willing it to ring with word of a new part that would be coming his way today, or tomorrow, or next week.

'Really, Hal,' my mother would say, over and over again. 'I am sure the right part for you will happen, but not if you keep standing guard over the telephone. Much better to go off and do something else, and the moment you get involved elsewhere, believe you me, the call will come. You are far too talented to be out of work for long.'

'My dear lady,' Hal finally boomed in return to this almost daily injunction, 'I wish that I could do something else, but I was born in a costume basket, backstage – Liverpool, I believe – and I have been trained for nothing more than acting, acting, acting. My father was an actor, my mother was an actress, and my grandparents too – all actors. I am part of a dynasty good for nothing else than becoming other people. Nothing to be done about it. I cannot now take up carpentry or welding. Or work as a postman. That would be like getting a fish to do ballet in the desert.'

I could see that he was rather pleased with his metaphor, but since the telephone then rang and he sprang up to get to it before Melville could, there was no time for him to savour his own cleverness.

As Melville's musical was still running he was less of a concern, but he still hurtled downstairs of a morning to get to the telephone before Hal, and Hal still had the agony of knowing that Melville was fully employed and likely to go on being so, while Hal might never get the right part again.

I supposed that there would be a change in his luck soon, as I also supposed that his day-to-day living costs were covered by the Office, but of course I didn't dare ask my father if this were so. However, I did ask him if we could help Hal in some new way.

'That was just what I was wondering,' my father said with sudden warmth. 'My thinking entirely, our Lottie.' He occasionally called me 'our Lottie' when he was feeling pleased with me; and having had a Yorkshire upbringing in a windy rectory, it suited him. It went with the pipe that he always smoked when in this particular mood.

He drew on his pipe for a while and there was the distinct sound of both of us wondering how to help Hal.

'Hal wanted to be recruited because he could never get into the Army on account of his faulty feet. His mother was always cramming them into ladies' shoes when he played girls in their touring company – as a consequence they are permanently bent. However, despite his missing out on National Service, I now feel he has given a great deal for his country in terms of his career. Theatre people, you know, they don't really hang around a flop like cats around a dustbin. Hal is off the lists of so many it is hard to see where to start.'

I thought about this. I liked to seize any and every opportunity to ingratiate myself with my father so I looked very concentrated, and allowed a long silence to elapse.

'Stands to reason that what he needs is to become more famous than he is now,' I volunteered. 'He needs to do something like throw himself in front of the Queen's horse.'

My father shook his head.

'Never ask the great British public to love you if you harm even so much as one hair of a horse or a dog, or even a cat for that matter, let alone the Queen's horse … but I do understand what you are saying. You are reaching towards some bold act that will start people talking about *Our Hal*.'

It was true. I was thinking about how Hal could become really famous, but not coming up with anything. I left my father with his pipe and, since I could smell baking, went downstairs to get some cake because

Mrs Graham was busy cooking for one of my mother's ladies' teas. Her chocolate cake being something special, I was preparing to wheedle her into making one for the Commander, who was such a good egg I felt he deserved it.

A few days later, after I returned from MI5, my father called me into his study. He had on his grimly excited expression, which usually signified grim excitement to come.

'I have had quite an exciting idea.' I looked reverential, because that always went down rather well. 'Yes,' he said after one of his very long pauses, which it was always unwise to interrupt. 'Yes. The idea is that we should help Hal by starting up a new extreme left-wing party, which he would head.'

I frowned. This idea, with due respect to my father's experience in spy-work, didn't sound very exciting. It seemed more like the Steerforth Notion, a bit on the dullish side.

'How would that go?' I asked, feeling for eggshells beneath my feet. 'I mean, for instance, what would you call it?'

'Something with Work in it — yes, that always goes down well.'

'Always,' I agreed, a little helplessly, because I was now well out of my depth. 'How about the Working Man's Party? 'Specially since Hal isn't working at the moment. It will give him motivation, and actors like that, they like motivation. I read about it last week in an interview with Marlon Brando.'

My father drew slowly on his pipe once more; finally he nodded.

'That could be a good name for it, Lottie,' he agreed. 'The Working Man's Party says what it is, and it sounds a cut above the Communist Party, which is difficult to identify with, if you think about it. Yes, the Working Man's Party could appeal to anyone, and everyone – even women.'

'You will have to have an organ, won't you?' I suggested with sudden authority. 'A newspaper, say, or a pamphlet. All political parties need those. Somewhere the members can air their extreme views, and feel better for it.'

'And the newspaper should be full of the sounds of strife going unrewarded,' my father agreed. 'In fact, that's what we'll call it – their paper – we'll call it *Strife*. Strife is always good. So, we have Working Man, and Strife. This has the makings of a grand plan. We're almost there. Now we just have to put it to Hal.'

I thought nothing would come of it, or that it would be like the Steerforth Notion, something that came and went without too much incident, but I was proved dreadfully wrong. I was to discover that when my father made a plan, he carried it through with almost alarming precision. He might not be the best burglar in the world, but he was always pleased if he could bring off something surprising, and judging from the gleam in his eye and the spring in his step, starting his own political party was to his way of thinking the undercover plan to beat all undercover plans.

He must have talked Hal into it because over the next weeks there were more low mutterings around the house than usual, and Mrs Graham was in a better mood because Hal now arose from his bed at a normal hour, which meant she could make it before teatime and that always pleased her, but that was before she opened her newspaper and read about him.

'I am very surprised at your father allowing this man to lodge here, Miss Lottie,' she told me, tapping the newspaper.

I read with fascination that Henry Flanagan, a member of the Flanagan acting dynasty, was heading a new political organisation called the Working Man's Party.

'I don't know what he knows about working,' Mrs Graham added with sudden astringency. 'He doesn't even make his own bed.'

Now it was there in print, I couldn't help feeling shocked. Hal of all people was being touted as the kind of person who would have a file in the Section, or worse — his file would be in a special place, one where you had to show your pass three times before — in years yet to come — you could open it wearing special white gloves.

'I expect it is just a passing phase,' I said. 'He's out of work so he has to think of something to do, so he's gone political.'

Mrs Graham made a 'humph' noise, but then a determined look came into her eyes.

'From now on,' she announced, 'the leader of the Working Man's Party can make his own bed.'

My mother was no less dubious.

'I hope this isn't one of your father's schemes,' she muttered. 'He will have them, and Hal has been hanging around the house for so long he might have felt he should think up something for him. Oh, well, just so long as Hal doesn't bring any Working Men back here, we should be all right.'

I became anxious to see how Hal would take his newfound fame. He took to it at once. I could hear my father rehearsing him in his rousing speeches that, following the example of Bernard Shaw, were to be made on street corners. *Strife* too was to be handed out, a pamphlet that my father wrote with great zeal, making constant use of the word *decadent*. *Profiteering* came into it too quite a lot, as well as *capitalism,* naturally. It was what he called 'strong stuff'.

Melville remained his usual charming self, singing and playing whenever the moment presented itself, but I noticed that he and Hal rarely talked now. There was more than a chasm between them: there was a whole world. Melville was not the kind of man to voice an opinion but he could certainly show his aversion.

'Of course nothing is going to come of it,' my mother announced as Hal, battered and blown by his street-corner orations, fell into Dingley Dell clutching some shredded copies of *Strife*.

'So you keep saying, dear lady,' he boomed. 'Meanwhile perhaps your delightful daughter would be good enough to fetch me some sticking plaster, some hot water, and a large whisky.'

My mother knew where her patriotic duty lay, and she sent me to fetch what was required, while Hal, on good dramatic form, groaned so much and so loudly that he could have been heard in Moscow.

'The great British public when roused turns into a fearsome beast,' he announced. 'I am fast coming to the realisation that the average working man does not like to be appealed to. He wants to be left alone to form his own ideas, and quite frankly I don't blame him.'

My mother nodded. She thought the same as the average working man, and I could see that she was hoping Hal's political flurry was now coming to a shuddering halt.

And so it might have done had not my father decided to bring Melville into the picture, and Melville decided that the whole idea needed opening out, and Hal preaching on street corners was not enough. They should have meetings.

'Not here, surely?' my mother asked in some desperation.

'Just to start with,' my father said, at his most nonchalant. 'One or two supporters for Hal, but nothing to write home about.'

And he lit his pipe and walked off.

'He's been reading too many of those Maigret novels in French again,' my mother said, looking irritated. 'You can always tell from what he's smoking. If it's John Buchan novels then he sticks to cigarettes. If it's Sherlock Holmes or Maigret, then out comes the pipe.'

'What about cigars?' I asked, although I had never seen him smoke one.

'That would be the Bible,' she said shortly. 'And he only reads that in bed.'

She sat down suddenly on a kitchen chair, which was only appropriate since we were in the kitchen.

'Oh dear, Lottie, what am I to do? Your father wants me to entertain supporters of this Working Man's Party, but I daren't ask Mrs Graham — she won't even make Melville's bed now ... won't go in either lodger's room. She says she sees them both as enemies of decent people. Their rooms are beginning to look like something from the war.'

I could see her predicament.

'Well, how about a running buffet?' I asked brightly. 'They always go down well with a mix of people.'

My mother thought for a minute.

'It's a long time since I cooked, Lottie, as you know, but a running buffet does sound a good idea. I could get out my old recipe books and make a lot of different dishes and then, as you say, people could help themselves, couldn't they?'

When I told Arabella she looked at me strangely.

'How long since your mother cooked?' she asked.

I thought for a minute.

'She always does cheese on toast on Sunday night. My father sometimes does conjuring tricks then to cheer up my grandmother, and it's Mrs Graham's evening off – not that she likes to take it because she says it makes more work because my mother leaves cheese everywhere.'

'Well, you can only hope,' Arabella said with some finality. 'Frankly, if her cooking is anything like Rosalie's, the running buffet is going to live up to its name – people will be running from it.'

'We don't want that,' I said, with some feeling. 'We want it to be a success.'

'Why isn't Mrs Graham doing the cooking?'

'She's on holiday for a day or two,' I said, too hastily.

Of course Arabella didn't believe me, but since we both knew that there was all too much in our lives about which we could never speak, and since I had no idea whether or not she knew that her mother was a double agent and the luxurious flat they lived in paid for by the Office, further conversation was at an end.

Invitations to the running buffet must have been sent out pretty quickly because my mother was soon having to cater for a great many more people than she would have wished. But for once she could not complain as my father pointed out that she had always wanted to have a busy social life and now she had one.

'Yes, but not this sort of social life. For the life of me, I never wanted to entertain a whole lot of working men whom I have never met before. It is hardly ideal, and I only hope that there will be some women too.'

The evening of the buffet arrived and my mother called me down to help with the food.

'It's all in there,' she said, nodding nervously towards the dining room as if there was a large dead animal laid out on the table. 'Just go and check everything, Lottie, would you? I think I have covered all eventualities'

I stared at the buffet. Remembering Arabella's words, I turned for the door. This was indeed an assembly of food to run from. Then I turned back. I could not hurt my mother's feelings. She had done her best. She had even made labels on cocktail sticks so that people knew what they were eating, which would probably be most alarming but it was too late to say anything.

'Well, what do you think?' she asked, looking both anxious and vulnerable.

'I think,' I said, 'that is a jolly good running buffet. Well done.'

She looked so happy at that.

'I was suddenly inspired,' she told me in a confidential tone, 'because I remembered the wartime recipes of Marguerite Patten, and all the rest of them. Brilliant recipes, everything disguised to look and taste like the real thing. I even remembered rhubarb jelly, and although it came out looking a bit grey, it certainly has the authentic wartime taste. You must try the snow foam made without egg, and rissoles made with marrow – add a dollop of mustard and you are in heaven. These wartime cooks were so inventive. They had to be.'

The Working Man's supporters looked exactly as anyone would expect, all seeming as if they had come straight from work, which I found oddly reassuring, yet at the same time I felt guilty because after all they were supporting my invention, and my invention was just a put up job to help Hal get lots of publicity so theatre managements would take him on for his shock value, and everyone could feel happy that they had done their bit to support the theatre and defeat communism too – although how that bit came into it, I wasn't quite sure.

Happily my father's drinks cupboard, unlike the buffet, was not in wartime mode. He dished out what he called a decent drink to all comers, and they were soon in a very jolly state, and what with Melville playing the piano and Hal singing 'The Red Flag', as well as lots of beer-drinking songs too, the whole evening had started off better than could have been hoped. My mother had persuaded me to wear a black dress and borrow one of Mrs Graham's white half-aprons, which seemed like a nice touch until I realised – all too late – that as far as working men were concerned waitresses and maids were fair game, so it was a case of duck and weave to avoid their attentions.

Finally everyone went downstairs to serve themselves at the buffet table. The moment they went in a terrible silence fell. My mother looked across at me, all anxiety.

'Come on, everyone, tuck in,' I said, in my usual Girl Guide over-bright way.

They took their plates like prisoners about to help themselves to thin gruel.

'All wartime recipes,' my mother announced, spooning rissoles on to their plates. 'Such clever people those wartime radio cooks, weren't they?'

Well, I don't know whether they were just being polite, but at her words those would-be supporters of the Working Man's Party looked quite differently at the buffet, and in a moment they were happily helping themselves. It seemed that as soon as they read the labels on the cocktail sticks memories came flooding back, and whether it was the rissoles or the runny rhubarb jelly, the eggless snow pudding or the kipper *pâté* made without kipper, the buffet became a centrepiece of enjoyment. Conversation around it became almost as noisy as the singing had been.

'What happens now?' I asked my father when everyone had gone. 'Do they have to sign things and make vows of allegiance to Hal?'

My father frowned. He was quite tired from helping my mother and me wash up, which was not something he was used to.

'It all depends on how things go on the streets,' he said. 'Movements like these depend on the street, and on enthusiasm from the ground upwards.' He lit a cigarette, from which I gathered he must have finished with Maigret and gone back to *The Thirty-Nine Steps*. 'The thing is, Hal is getting a lot of bad publicity, and that is very good, just what is needed. All the right-wing papers are very suspicious of anyone who shows enthusiasm for the working man, as they always have been. As far as the right wing is concerned, the Working Man's Party must be bad news because they are never sure whether the Working Man is actually on their side or not. They live in fear of the Working Man the way the Army live in fear of their own men, because most officers can't wire a plug or change a washer in a tap. I know I can't, but I'm not right-wing or left-wing. I simply don't want the communists taking over and making our lives less British.'

I knew my father must be one over the eight because he didn't usually talk like that, so I went to bed feeling rather thoughtful. The evening had been a great success, but was that what was wanted? Shouldn't all the Working Men have sat down and parleyed politics rather than reminiscing about the war on account of my mother's food?

As things were life in the Section was toddling along at such a slow pace that I had started to wonder if there were any communists left in England, because none of the files were very fat, and Commander Steerforth's dictation was slower than ever, and in contrast to the files he was beginning to put on so much weight from my supplying him with cakes.

I didn't dare ask Hal how things were going because he might tell me the truth, and I was in no mood to hear it, so I asked Melville, who was now on side with Hal as they knew but couldn't say that they were both spooks. Melville had even attended the buffet, posing as a supporter of the new political movement.

'The Party was going fine until that night,' he told me gravely while adjusting his immaculate Garrick Club tie and pulling his white shirt cuffs down to exactly the required Savile Row level, exposing gold cufflinks. 'But then, everything changed.'

I stared at him, imagining all those poor people going home with tummy aches.

'What happened after that? To make it all change.'

Melville looked grave.

'Well, I was sent to canvass them, which I duly did. That is, I took their telephone numbers and addresses before they left and then I followed up. It was amazing.' He shook his head. 'It was the buffet, Lottie. They were all so impressed your mother had made such an effort for them that they changed their minds about joining a new political movement. It was all the wartime memories – put them off party politics completely. We were united then, with everyone pulling their weight. Political squabbles are just shabby in comparison. So that, I am afraid, is that.'

'How do you mean?'

'I mean, Lottie, that there are some things more important than politics, such as making people the right food, and your mother has proved it. She is a brilliant woman, and I have told her so. Brilliant.'

I must say, for once in my life I was lost for words. Normally I can think of something, but then I simply couldn't.

'So, if the movement has been a bit of a damp squib, what will Hal do?' I finally asked.

Melville looked surprised that I didn't know.

'Hasn't anyone told you? He has had any number of offers to star in any number of plays; we might even be in one together – if my dates fit. No, Hal is right up there now, and of course before too long he will have an in-depth interview in the *Sunday Express* in which he will announce that he has reformed his ways, as a consequence of which everyone will crowd the theatres to see him because – quite simply – he is now properly famous.'

I sighed with some relief. There were happy endings after all.

And then I thought of something.

'What about Dame Lily, has she got any work?'

'The Bard has come to her rescue, as always,' Melville said, moving towards the drawing-room piano because, as he had told me, he became restless if he was in the room with a piano and wasn't playing it. 'Dame Lily has been offered the Nurse in *R and J*.'

I went to my father's drink cupboard, and as Melville played I sipped my young wine, and suddenly felt older.

SMOKIN' FISH

Now that Hal was in work, and everyone at Dingley Dell well satisfied that they had done their best to help him while still maintaining the fight against communism, the house settled down to a routine. In line with my father's new policy of defeating communist infiltration in entertainment, our visitors were mainly actors and what he called *show business types,* coming and going. Some vaguely countrified types also came and went, as well as my brother, who was stationed abroad in the army and so only occasionally visited. It was a happy atmosphere, and after all the strain of the previous weeks and months, everything seemed set fair.

Such was not the case in our Section, however. Commander Steerforth was if anything more gloomy, and even Rosalie was showing signs of strain. The truth was there was very little work to do. Yes, there was *work* but it was not showing any results. We were all feeling a bit like out-of-work actors who have memorised their roles and are word perfect but have nowhere to demonstrate their skills because suddenly there's no show.

It was Arabella who put it best.

'We are simply not trapping enough communist agents or people selling secrets to foreigners, and that is the truth of it. We type reports, we file them, but what do we have to show for it? Not a double agent in sight at the moment. Of course, we know there are some creepy intellectuals hiding behind respectable posts and using Top Secret material to help the Commies, but we are not flushing them out. We have nothing to show for all this shorthand and typewriter bashing.'

I looked at her, knowing exactly what she meant, and also knowing that she was right.

'I mean, when was the last time anyone was trapped? We couldn't even trap Sergei … remember him? Well, he is still hanging around my mother and still very trappable. That was a flop if ever there was one.'

I nodded while at the same time wondering whether Arabella knew what her mother was, and how brave and invaluable she had been to the Service.

'I told Rosalie about Sergei and so on, but she said he was too useful where he was, so that was that. You would have thought they would have wanted to put a trace on him, but no. And as for Mater, she wouldn't hear of him being anything except a very nice young man who missed his mother in Moscow and liked taking Mater to concerts.'

So that was my question answered. Arabella knew nothing about Mater being a double agent – unless she was even cleverer than I knew her to be.

'We need to cheer the Section up,' I said, in an effort to change the subject.

Arabella shook her head.

'No more of your posters. They lasted all of five minutes if you remember – before Head of Section had them taken down.'

'No, I was thinking more like running a book. My brother is always running a book in his regiment. He gives odds and acts like a bookmaker and it turns out really well for him. The Grand National, Cheltenham, the Queen's birthday parade.'

'How on earth do you bet on the Queen's birthday parade?'

'Simple. You bet on, say, how many minutes until the first guardsman faints.'

At that Arabella looked sphinx-like, which was always a sign.

'That could be good,' she conceded.

There the matter rested, because I knew never to crowd her since it wasn't her style. If the idea took she would come up with something, which she duly did over tea in the canteen.

'You know how Rosalie smokes?' she asked, stirring her tea with the personal spoon that for some reason she always carried.

'I know she smokes, yes,' I replied with caution.

'Yes, but do you know how she smokes?'

'Same as everyone else?' I suggested. 'She puts a cigarette in her mouth and lights up.'

'Exactly so,' Arabella agreed, and she slowly – very slowly and really very decorously – took a sip of her tea, holding the cup in her left hand. 'She takes a cigarette from her cigarette case and she lights up. But that is not all. By no means. Rosalie being Rosalie, and let us face it that means a little vague, she seems to forget she has said cigarette in her mouth in spite of the fact she is smoking it, so the ash lasts and lasts until finally it falls – usually on a more than interesting SF.'

'Oh,' I said. 'So she doesn't believe in ashtrays?'

I knew Arabella was fastidious, but this was verging on the boring.

'So,' she said, eyes glinting with excitement, 'taking you up on your idea, *my* idea is to run a book on how long it takes for the ash to drop.'

I was overcome with admiration. This was just the kind of thing to cheer up the Section.

'But how will we entice her out of her office into the big room with a cigarette going so that we can see who wins?'

'I've thought of that.' Arabella wiped her personal silver spoon and popped it back into her handbag. 'I will put one of the more important SFs in a tray outside her office and pretend it needs checking. I will have to do it the moment she lights up. She is such a sport she will follow me out and have a dekko at it, which is when the fun can start. It will have to be something long, but that's not difficult.'

'What size bets will you take?'

'Any size, but nothing below two shillings.'

'The odds?' I asked.

'I will announce them later,' she said shortly.

I couldn't help feeling excited, but as we left the canteen I had to ask her something I had wanted to ask for some time.

'Why do you always use your left hand when you're drinking, when you're really right-handed?'

Arabella looked surprised.

'Stands to reason,' she said, sighing and giving me a patronising look. 'Most people are right-handed, so there are more germs on that side of glasses and cups. If you drink left-handed you avoid most of them. Why did you think?'

'Nothing, really. I just wondered.'

I did not tell her that my father did the same thing but for rather different reasons. He used his left hand to hold his glass in order to leave his gun hand free.

Back in the Section we started to put our plan into action. Everyone came in on the betting, and at once the mood in the place started to lighten. Now all that had to happen was for Arabella to leave the file in full view of the rest of us, so we could time Rosalie's cigarette ash.

Sure enough out came the magnificent sight of Rosalie complete with freshly lit smokey.

'Arabella?' she called. 'Is this the file you are so worried about?'

Arabella, unable to leave her position behind her Underwood typewriter, called back, 'Yes, Miss Lovington!' her eyes not moving from her watch.

Seconds went by, then further seconds, while the ash lengthened and lengthened as Rosalie, with that particular expertise that confirmed smokers have, let it hang in place while she read through the important file.

Oh, the agony of it. I had five shillings on its being twenty seconds, and thought I must be on to a winner, but no, on went the reading, and on grew the ash, until finally, as she closed the file, the ash fell.

No sooner had it done so than an audible cheer went up from Files because they had pooled their resources and consequently won a great many shillings. Commander Steerforth dashed out of his office, Rosalie looked astonished, and Arabella flew up from behind her desk.

'Have we caught someone?' Commander Steerforth asked, hope rising in his voice.

'No, no, it's just Doreen,' Arabella improvised, nodding at one of her friends in Files. 'She's finished her jumper at last.'

Doreen waved her completed work obligingly, and everyone laughed.

'Well done, Doreen,' said Commander Steerforth, and putting his brave face back on, returned to his office.

'Yes, well done, Doreen,' said Rosalie, and rather affectingly she went over and patted her on the shoulder. 'Good work. Knitting was the backbone of the country during the war. Can't do without stalwarts like you.'

So all told that was a great success, and Arabella was rightly pleased, but despite demand from everyone in the Section, it was not something that could be repeated because, as Arabella announced sadly a few days later, Rosalie had decided to give up smoking in favour of snuff.

I thought for a minute.

'You could run a book on how often she sneezes,' I suggested.

Arabella shook her head.

'Not so easy. Besides, she said something about only doing it out of office hours, so that would be no good.'

However, as can happen, sometimes one thing leads to another. After I confessed to my father that the work in our Section was very slow and very dull, he looked thoughtful.

'I'll think of something for you, if you like,' he said, moving towards Melville, who was playing his favourite number from a recent musical.

'Oh, dear, I do hope he doesn't,' my mother sighed above the sound of the music and the singing. 'Life always gets so complicated when your father thinks of something.'

I myself thought no more about it, until Arabella came into the Section looking less serene than usual.

'My mother has been asked to go and stay with friends in America, and she's in a bit of a fluff because Sergei has been recalled to Moscow to look after his mother. She thinks that's going to be the end of the vodka and the caviar. Sergei's having a nervous breakdown, and now I've seen a photo of his mother I'm not surprised.'

We both started to type and for a few minutes there was nothing to be heard in the Section except the sound of Underwoods being bashed.

Arabella stopped bashing after a few minutes.

'Look,' she said, 'since I'm going to be on my own in the flat for the summer months while Mater is away, why don't you come and stay at the old place with me? Make a change from your parents and all those actors and so on, wouldn't it? And I mean, it is so much nearer Harrods.'

I thought about it for a few seconds, and then remembering that Mater was a double agent working for our side as well as for their side, and reckoning Sergei was probably the same, but not knowing what to say for the best, I trod water.

'I'd better ask my father, and my mother, of course,' I added quickly so as not to sound as if I had any suspicions at all. 'I'm not needed at home except for Mr and Mrs Graham's annual holiday and they haven't taken one of those for years on account of the seaweed at Worthing smelling so dreadful.'

I went home and waited for my father in my usual way – that is to say, I waited until he had handed out an inordinate amount of drinks to everyone and anyone and then I asked him if it was all right for me to go and stay at Mater's flat.

His eyes lit up in their own special way – that is he looked at me, and then looked away, and then he looked at me again.

'Splendid idea,' he said. 'Couldn't be better.'

'Oh, good,' I said, and then I moved nearer him, which I knew he wouldn't like but it was necessary with so many other people in the room. 'You know about ahem leaving for ahem, don't you?'

He nodded.

'Yes, that was all arranged some time ago,' he replied. 'Seems his mother, you know – poor soul – needs looking after.' He started to walk away. 'Yes, you move in with Arabella while her mother is out of the country, and have a good time of it. I know you will.'

He turned and winked at me.

I should have known then that there was more to this than he was going to say because my father never, ever did anything such as *wink*. Looking back, it was probably the signal that he gave his agents when he wanted them to be on the alert, or to move forward a hundred paces and open fire. I really had no idea. All I was for the moment was astonished, when actually what I should have been was uneasy.

My mother, of course, was pleased, because it meant she could have someone to stay in my room, so she even helped me pack up, and within a few days I found myself living in the unusual setting of total luxury.

The difference between our house and Mater's apartment – you couldn't really call it a flat – was the difference between everyday jam-along living and moving into the Ritz. I had only been dimly aware that Arabella lived in such comfort, but now I was alive to it.

It was not just the snowy carpets, the bedrooms filled with luxurious fabrics, the curtains so thick that not even the sound of a Harrods electric van could be heard – it was the sheer detail of it. I had never seen such large bottles of scent and bath toiletries, soap with French names, and sponges so big that bathtime invited dreams of South Sea Islands and expectations of turtles swimming towards the bath plug.

There was only one luxury missing, and that was the foreign maid.

'Maria Constanza – has she gone to the US of A with Mater?'

Arabella shook her head.

'I don't suppose Maria Constanza would be allowed into America,' she said succinctly. 'No, she never stays here when Mater is on the hoof, because then she can't make enough money at the back door out of selling the stuff she over-orders on Mater's accounts, which means that she is out of pocket. It is a dreadful shame, because she is quite useful at making beds and dreadful coffee, but Mater has asked one of the agencies to send in someone in Maria Constanza's stead, while she goes off to fill in as a temp in St James's or somewhere like that. Whoever they send from the agency in her place, let's hope they make better coffee.' At half-past seven the next morning the front doorbell rang, and Arabella, who was in the adjoining bedroom, woke me up. I was rather annoyed to be woken so early as it was Saturday, my day for a sleep in and dressing-gown order at breakfast.

'Who do you think that is? Not Sergei, I hope?' I asked, sitting up.

We both pulled on our dressing gowns and, for no reason at all, I grabbed an umbrella from the hall stand while Arabella cautiously opened the front door, with the chain still on.

'*Hallooo?*' our visitor cooed from the other side. '*Halloo?* I'm from the agency – Monty from the Agency? I expect they rang and told you?'

We both looked at each other. Surely no Sergei-type person calling themself Monty would come calling at seven-thirty in the morning wearing a little white coat? Arabella closed the door and undid the chain.

Monty – if it was indeed he, which it turned out it was – stood facing us, and slowly raised what was on his head, namely his hair, and then just as slowly replaced it.

'Good morning, ladies, Monty at your service. I am here to take the place of Maria Unpronounceable, as we all call her.' Since he had replaced his toupe a little crooked Arabella was forced to flee to the bathroom from which she did not emerge for some minutes, leaving me to show him to the kitchen, and his own lodgings.

'Very nice, very nice, and quite what one is used to,' he told me. 'I always say it is worth waiting for the Upper Echelons to engage you because they know how to treat you – comfy beds and plenty of what have you when you want it, if you get my meaning.'

I didn't quite, but I thought I knew what he meant.

'If you move further down the Echelons, it's just Marmite sandwiches for supper and endless fish forks to polish. Now take me to the kitchen and the cleaning cupboards and I shall be in heaven.'

Happily for me, Arabella had recovered herself and was able to show Monty where everything was kept.

'Oh, Jemima, there's more vodka and caviar here than in Stalin's old dachau,' he crooned, opening the doors of the huge Bendix refrigerator.

'It was for my mother's old secretary. He liked vodka and caviar.'

'All right if you can get it, ducks,' Monty said, tugging at something under his white jacket. 'Now you both shoo while I assemble breakfast. Shoo, shoo, off you go, and no argufying.'

As we retired to our bedrooms to dress, Arabella nodded back to the now closed kitchen door.

'I don't like it, Lottie. He's too odd. If you ask me he could easily be working for the other side.' She added with cool professionalism, 'Have you seen his shape?'

I had noticed Monty's shape, of course, and it was decidedly odd, but then quite a lot of people were oddly shaped, and I never like to dwell on something unpleasant for too long.

'He could have anything you could name under that white jacket of his, given that shape. He could be concealing things we wouldn't like.'

This made me feel nervous.

'He showed me his agency card.'

'Anyone could get hold of one of those, especially if they're foreign. You just have to hang about Knightsbridge looking dubious. I'm sure he's a plant – and as for all that business about Stalin, that was a bit spooky, wasn't it?'

I knew I had spies on the brain, but I hadn't realised that Arabella was in the same condition.

'Best if we do as he says, and we should also get dressed before breakfast,' I said to change the subject, remembering how upset Mrs Graham became whenever she found Hal still in his pyjamas answering the telephone to his agent.

Arabella agreed that it was the best plan and some minutes later I found myself following her as she pushed open the green baize door that led to the kitchen. We both stopped short when we saw the kitchen table. It was laid with breakfast china, and everything on it was perfection. The marmalade even had a spoon, and Monty was at the kitchen range cooking what smelled like the perfect fried breakfast.

I looked across at him adoringly. There was no other word for it. The fact was that I never felt hungry on a weekday, but come Saturday morning and I could eat as hearty as a man who had galloped ten miles without a saddle or a bridle.

'Tell Monty what you would like, petal.' He turned and gave my chair a quick polish before I sat down.

'I would like eggs, bacon, sausage and fried bread,' I said in a dreamy voice.

'Eggs sunny side up?'

'Any side up,' I said, happily.

I had never been asked that before, and had only ever heard anyone saying it in a film.

'I would like scrambled eggs, crispy bacon, and fingers on the side, thank you.'

I knew that Arabella prided herself on her ability not to get excited about anything but I could see that even she was feeling that genuine excitement that being looked after properly always brings.

The breakfast seemed to appear effortlessly, and beautifully. I was astonished by how good it tasted, it made me feel as if I had been taken into a different world – and what with Monty occasionally flapping the napkin he kept over his shoulder as well as constantly humming a Noël Coward song, I just wanted breakfast to continue for the rest of my life.

'Do you think he's a friend of Sergei's?' Arabella wondered later, when we had repaired to Harrods to look at very expensive luggage, which we both preferred to do rather than at dresses, because as Arabella always said they never asked you if you wanted to try on luggage.

'He could be a friend of anyone's,' I said with some feeling. 'I mean someone who cooks a breakfast as good as that must have more friends than the Queen.'

'I do like those, don't you?'

I pointed at an open suitcase; half of which was designed as a wardrobe and the other half for folded garments.

'They are the best.'

I could see Arabella wasn't as enthused as she normally was in the luggage department, so we drifted on to picnic cases, but again she was not really concentrating.

Finally she confessed when we went for a coffee: 'I think I might be right. Monty could well be a spy.'

I sighed inwardly. This was how MI5 got at its employees, however humble. They made you think that there was someone at every corner either listening in or, in the case of Monty, serving you breakfast

'Oh, no, surely not? Anyway,' I thought for a minute, 'spies don't really cook, not as well as that.'

'How do you know?'

I didn't, of course, but since my friendships with Melville and Hal I had the feeling that I was becoming a bit of an expert on agents.

Arabella leaned forward, lowered her voice and then said the one thing I had been dreading.

'The thing is, Lottie, for a long time now I have had a horrid feeling that my mother is one too. That is why I think Monty is probably one as well, and of course Sergei. I think my mother is working for the Russians and that is why there is so much vodka and caviar about the place. It's a thought that must have plagued you as well? Do admit it.'

I wondered quickly what my father would have me say to this, and promptly came up with what I can only describe as a conversational double back clip.

'If your mother were working for the Russians, she would not be so careless about the vodka and the caviar and letting Sergei take her to concerts. I mean she wouldn't be so overt, would she? And under those circumstances, she could not be going to stay with friends near the Pentagon because that is somewhat overt as well.'

I could see that Arabella was impressed by this line of thought.

'But still,' she said finally, 'that doesn't mean Monty isn't a spook.'

'Spies don't cook like that,' I said, sticking to my guns. 'Besides he wants us to pick up something for him from that corset shop opposite, so that too is a bit overt. I mean no spook would want us to pick up something for him from there if they were busy being undercover, would they? They would keep their corset orders, or whatever it is he wants us to get, to themselves, wouldn't they?'

'What would he want us to go there for?'

'It's something for his mother's birthday actually. It's all paid for.'

We duly picked up the parcel in question and although I knew that we were both itching to open it, we also knew without saying so that we would never be able to pack it back together again.

Monty snatched the parcel, and almost ran off with it to his quarters, which made Arabella give me her did-you-see-that look, before laying aside all suspicions about him in order to devour the lunch of fried trout with almonds and lemon mousse that he set before us. After which, now full of both breakfast and lunch, she fell asleep on the deeply upholstered drawing-room sofa, only to be woken by the telephone which rang just twice, before being picked up elsewhere.

'A company called Trigata called and wanted to know our orders, so I asked them what they had in fresh and they said salt cod and pickled herring,' Monty reported. '"No, I don't think so," I said. Something to go with this Sergei's taste in vodka, I suppose.'

As he turned to leave I privately wondered if salt cod and pickled herring were perhaps code words, and if so what they stood for.

'Oh, thank you, Monty, very kind of you, and you're quite right – neither salt cod nor pickled herring would be to our taste. No need to take any more calls for us, we can answer the telephone ourselves, really we can. We are both trained secretaries,' Arabella told him.

I knew that Commander Steerforth had cross-referenced Trigata and duly come up with what could be matters of grave interest to the state. Trigata imported and exported any number of items, and they were of course a cover, but no one could quite discover what kind of cover, or for whom, or why.

This was where being on our own in Mater's flat could come in useful.

The whole matter came to a head on Monday, and it was Monty who set alarm bells ringing in my head.

'If,' he said, slinging his little wickerwork shoulder bag on a string over one shoulder, 'Trigata rings again, tell them it is still no to salt cod and pickled herring, and do make sure to insist on that – because they will not take no for an answer. And they sound so foreign it's enough to make you think they're up to no good. Thick foreign accents are not what is wanted, let alone salt cod and pickled herring. Dear me, before we turn round they will be dancing to "The Red Flag" at a Buckingham Palace ball.'

'If Trigata rings when you're out, Monty – we will order and see what happens,' Arabella replied, a deter-mined look in her eyes.

'I shouldn't bother, Miss Arabella. I mean today I put in an order for lobster because Harrods was out, but that seemed to send them right up the pole and back down again. They kept shouting at me they didn't have lobster! They didn't have any something lobster. They were being really tiresome about it.'

Of course I couldn't tell Arabella about Commander Steerforth and the trace, or the file that had nothing in it, so I just quickly flicked through a copy of the *Tatler* which was on a nearby table and wished that I could be smart like the people in it, who were seemingly quite unaware of the huge lengths that people like Arabella and I went to protect them from being called decadent because they liked wine and nice frocks.

The next day I suggested to Commander Steerforth that we send for the Trigata file, particularly since at the moment there was nothing in it. We might add to it with details of the calls to Mater's flat. It seemed a good thing to do, so we sent for the file, and in it came, but it was no longer thin.

'We seem to have a great deal of new info about Trigata,' Commander Steerforth said excitedly. 'You can see from this recent intercept an order has come up mentioning lobsters – which apparently is setting all sorts of alarm bells ringing – and when one looks at what that code word means, one can understand why. I tell you, *lobsters* is serious stuff, Lottie. By that I mean *lobsters*,' he added with a meaningful look, which I'm afraid meant nothing to me. '*Lobsters,* Lottie? *Lobsters?*' he repeated, now adding a mime for what I took to be inverted commas.

I realised at once that in this case all roads were not leading to Rome, and found myself wondering if I should perhaps come clean and confess as much to Commander Steerforth.

'Actually the lobsters were for our dinner tonight,' I explained. 'The chap who is helping at the flat ordered them.' As Commander Steerforth looked interested I went on: 'He was so fed up with Trigata ringing us up day in, day out, constantly asking if we wanted salt cod and pickled herring, that he decided to annoy them and ordered lobster.'

Commander Steerforth looked impressed.

'That will have put them all in a complete panic,' he said. 'As you will see from the decoding here, Trigata's only really been dealing in salt cod and herring, importing the stuff all over the place, so they will be rocking in their boat after this particular order.' He looked serious. 'I wonder whether we should go ahead and have them deliver the lobster?'

'But that is just the point, Commander,' I said, panicked by the thought of what this might do to our proposed dinner. 'If they have no lobster, only salt cod and herring, then shouldn't we really leave it at that?'

'Well, lobster is a very dangerous new path for Trigata to be embarking on. We are having a bad enough time, spotting where the salt cod and the herring are going and stopping them before they do any harm.'

'Tell you what,' I said, ever helpful. 'Next time they ring, I'll make sure we cancel the lobster order.'

'In the interests of everyone concerned, I think perhaps that might be best.'

That evening, after supper, I told Arabella to tell Monty to make sure to cancel the order, and we sat down to listen to the radio and varnish our toenails, which is always such a job.

'Oh, I already told him – but, you know, it's very strange,' she said, looking up from her toes. 'Monty is convinced Trigata is nothing to do with fish at all. He thinks they're something much more sinister on account of the thick foreign accents and Sergei and all that vodka.'

I nodded.

'He might be right,' I said, trying to cover the mark on the sofa where I had spilled some varnish. 'Trigata could be a cover for anything.'

'Who knows?' she wondered. 'Monty might have well and truly set the cat among the pigeons. I mean supposing *lobster* is code for something much more sinister? You know – like – like guns, say? Or grenades? Or even maybe missiles?'

I gave a forced laugh.

'I know. Or supposing lobsters just means lobsters?'

'You're no fun when it comes to fantasies,' Arabella grumbled.

It was thinking about our intended dinner being a threat to everyone's safety that had made me a bit humourless, but I soon cheered up when I saw what Monty had made us instead – the most delicious-smelling *Boeuf Bourguignon* – better than any lobster surely?

Before we put our lights out Arabella shared her secret with me.

'I've worked out why Monty is such an odd shape,' she said.

'He's half man, half lobster?' I suggested.

'Because he wears ladies' corsets.'

'How sweet,' I said, and fell asleep wondering if perhaps I should tell Commander Steerforth this, but put it firmly out of my mind. Corsets might easily turn out to be code for something much more deadly. No, no, let Monty enjoy his corsets in peace, and leave us at MI5 to safeguard it.

WHY

It was a shame for everyone, especially me, when Mater came back early from the US of A. Her reason for returning was not clear, but I was sad to have to pack up and leave Arabella, Monty and Knightsbridge for downtown Kensington. I felt that everything that had happened at the apartment had changed me, but not as much as my bedroom at Dingley Dell had changed. It was now far more in the taste of Mater than my mother. The bedcover was chintzy and squishy, and the pillows, despite fresh linen, smelled distinctly of My Sin, a very fashionable scent that women who were not exactly ladies were prone to wear. I'd had barely enough time to hang up my clothes before my mother appeared.

'Your father has been auditioning plants,' she said, in a melancholy tone. 'You should see some of them – very exotic, verging on the tropical. It's to do with his work. Melville is advising him, but most of them seem to know Hal better than they know Melville.'

I was surprised. My father had always been adamant that exotic plants were no use to him. He needed to take on plants no one would suspect. The *Miss Smiths* of this world, he called them. But according to my mother, too many Miss Smiths planted in all sorts of left-leaning places had had their cover blown, and so a more exotic plant was now needed

'It's a real bother, *Why*—'

'Probably,' I said, determined to be reasonable, 'it's part of his stopping propaganda in the entertainment world – keep it all from being left-leaning. Much more *Passport to Pimlico* than *Family Fun in Siberia*.'

'No, Lottie, not why why – *Why* is the name of a new film directed by this chap Leslie Robertson. It is called *Why*, and is being directed by this very rich communist with left-wing views, who is determined to bring down the establishment from inside. This is why your father needed to audition all these plants, but none of them were any good for what he wanted. He needed a pretty young woman with shorthand and typing, but none of these ladies, if they could be called such, were good at anything except being pretty, which was only to be expected since they all seem to have been put up for the job by Hal.'

I felt sorry for my mother, who always bore the brunt at Dingley Dell, but at that moment I felt sorrier for myself, seemingly cemented into a very dull job. Rosalie had written such a glowing report about Arabella that she was now destined to leave our Section and go on to higher and greater things. To shake off my mood of self-pity, I asked her to Sunday lunch at Dingley Dell.

The usual cast were present and the atmosphere happy and jolly as Melville played some of my father's favourite tunes, while Hal boomed at my mother about some new playwright, who was due to have a play put on at the Royal Court Theatre.

'All scratch and spit, dear lady – not a decent line to be heard anywhere. I have a luckless friend in it who's in despair, but what can you do? He needs the work – like us all, he needs to be seen.'

'Just as well you have the film, Hal,' my mother was saying as Arabella and I came into the drawing room, and I went to the drinks cupboard for some wine.

I don't think Hal had paid much attention to my mother's words of comfort, because the moment he had clapped eyes on Arabella he became mesmerised. Of that there was no doubt. It was as if he had never seen her before. He moved towards her straight away. My mother, who was quite used to him by now, took it in good part.

'You know Lottie's friend Arabella, of course, Hal,' she said to his back as he abandoned her.

I gave Arabella a glass of wine and went over to the piano. It was not just my mother who was used to Hal and his ways — even Mrs Graham had given up on ever reforming him.

'This is serendipitous indeed,' Hal boomed at my father after lunch. 'We have found our Miss Smith, my dear sir — we have *found* her.'

Since by now Arabella had gone home and with my mother upstairs taking a siesta, and Melville back playing piano in the drawing room, there was no one else in the room but myself so Hal was able to speak his mind.

My father looked at him with something close to affection. He liked his new life among actors and, although I knew he worried when Hal got insanely drunk, he trusted him more than he did a great many of his other people.

'Who and what have you found, Hal?'

'Why — the pretty young lady who was just here! She does shorthand and typing — so in she goes to the production office, surely? Just the plant you were looking for — we were all looking for.' Hal looked as if he was about to doff an Elizabethan hat and bow to my father, he was so excited.

At first I could hardly believe what he was saying, and then I realised that he was right. Arabella would make the perfect plant. The unsuspecting production office — seething with Lefties according to Hal — would happily take on a beautiful young woman with shorthand speeds that could not be matched by many and hands that managed to fly over an old Underwood as if they were driving a Grand Prix racing car.

My father frowned. This was always a good sign.

'Arabella?' His frown grew deeper, another good sign. 'Do you know, I think you're right, Hal. She would be perfect. She can take compassionate leave and be moved in via one of our loyal theatrical agencies, keeping us informed from the inside.'

Hal beamed.

'Just one thing, Hal. I don't want anyone giving her a bottle of *My Sin*. Frightful stuff. I'd say it's got skunk in it.'

'Comfort yourself, sir, my job lot of that particular perfume has run out.'

'Just as well,' my father said, tersely. 'Mrs Graham was threatening to use DDT to drown it out, and that would never do.'

Now I saw the writing on the MI5 wall I suddenly felt depressed, something I usually avoid. I went up to my room and lay down on the bed. I had never really bothered to make any more friends in the Section, but now I would have to, for with Arabella gone I would have to find myself another canteen crony, and not even Commander Steerforth's devotion to cakes would alleviate the boredom of my day.

Arabella was soon on her way, the story being that she was taking a few weeks' leave to look after her ailing mother. Meanwhile I was to stand in for her as Commander Steerforth was also taking leave.

'I shall miss Arabella but hopefully she will soon be back. We need people like her in the Section,' Rosalie said, putting a Biro in her mouth in the same way that she used to put a cigarette there and speaking round it. 'Just tell me if I dictate too fast, won't you?'

Of course I knew Rosalie dictated like a snail on brandy, but I wasn't going to tell her that. I just smiled and hoped I would make a new friend in the Section to take the place of Arabella. Someone soon stopped by my Underwood.

'I expect you're missing Arabella, aren't you?'

I knew her name was Mary Claire. I also knew and admired her typing technique, which was stupendous because she had the most perfectly manicured nails I had ever seen. They would put a professional mani-curist to shame. Long and red, so long that she typed with flat fingers but at such a speed it was little short of extraordinary.

'Yes, I am missing Arabella. Shall we go for coffee?' I asked her, despite the fact that I can't ever help feeling suspicious of anyone who wants to be friends with me, always thinking they ought to be able to find someone better.

'Yes, all right,' she agreed, and we soon settled down to important matters such as where to have lunch.

Mary Claire was very different from Arabella. She never looked you in the eye, and was so restless I thought she might be in pain. Whereas Arabella was at pains always to seem composed, Mary Claire was quite the opposite: she could not even drink a coffee without getting up and changing the sugar on our table for the sugar on someone else's. She gazed around the room as if she was about to swap my company for someone else's, and worst of all, she smoked in a very unnerving way. She tapped the cigarette constantly against the tin ashtray. I found myself wishing I had never suggested having coffee with her, but it was an unwritten rule in the Section that once you agreed to go to coffee with someone, you were on the same side, probably for life.

All in all, except for Rosalie, who was an absolute dear, I was soon feeling quite down, and as usual my father seemed to sense this.

'Hal and I were wondering if you would like to be an extra on *Why?*' He lit a cigarette. 'You could take a week or two's leave and learn to mill about, or whatever they do, couldn't you? Section can move someone else in as usual. Means you'll get to see Arabella, you'll like that.'

I thought this sounded a suggestion from heaven. When should I start? What sort of extra would I be?

'The Lord alone knows,' my father said dolefully. 'Film folk hardly know what they're doing from one day to the next, and even then it's doubtful. I'll try and get you put down on the schedule for next week.'

I had to tell Rosalie and Mary Claire that I too was taking some leave to help out at home.

'I hope it isn't another of these sudden departures to look after a sick mother?' Rosalie observed. Then she said with some dread in her voice: 'Section Head is sending me Mary Claire, which is not what was wanted on voyage.'

I must have looked surprised, because I had never heard Rosalie be anything but kind.

'She has terrific speeds.'

Rosalie shook her head.

'She keeps stopping work to go for a gasper. I've seen her in the ladies', her head stuck out of the window, puffing away as if her life depended on it.'

'You could suggest snuff.'

'That's a good idea,' Rosalie agreed, brightening. 'Hope you have a good leave.'

'I don't suppose it will be.'

How wrong I had been I only realised the following morning when I shared Hal and Melville's chauffeur-driven car. They put me up in front beside the driver so they could talk in low voices about the director, the film, and possibly even Arabella.

At the studio everyone seemed to know where they were going, except for me. My father had not bothered to outline my job except to say that I was going to be an extra. I asked Melville as he was the last out of the car.

'I don't know, dear heart. One has never been an extra. Go to makeup, that's always safe. Everyone starts in makeup, and then waits to be told what to do next.'

I found makeup. It was being guarded by a burly-looking individual.

'Who are you?'

I told him.

'I haven't got you down here,' he said.

'Well, you should have,' I told him.

'Your name again?'

Once again I told him. Once again he failed to find me on his list.

'You can't go in there if you're not on the list.'

I looked at him, feeling suddenly angry. If it weren't for people like me he wouldn't have a list, I thought – probably wrongly – but then it was very early in the morning.

For no reason I know, and to this day I don't understand why I did it, I took out my MI5 pass and flashed it at him.

'Security,' I said, in what I hoped was a growly voice.

He almost bowed as he waved me past, and it was only when I was in the makeup area with all the lights and the people and the rest of it that I realised I would probably end up in the Tower because of what I had done, but somehow the whole show business atmosphere had got to me, and I knew without any doubt that I had entered the kind of world where anything could happen, and probably did.

'So what are we doing for this little miss today?' asked the makeup man.

'Just the usual,' I said, with assumed nonchalance.

He cast a look at me in the mirror.

'Are you in the party scene this morning?'

I really didn't know whether I was or not, so of course I nodded.

'I'll give you the same makeup I give Vivien Leigh,' he told me, his head tilted to one side as he stared at me. 'You remind me a little of her, the same small features — they need bringing out. But I'll lose your eyes. Your eyes are bigger than hers were, or are. Although I haven't done her since just before *Gone* … but I don't suppose the eyes have got any smaller.'

He worked away at me for what seemed like hours, and the more he worked the more miserable I felt. I had never liked makeup much and now I was being plastered in it, I liked it even less.

'Off you go, dear, and if I were you I'd ask for a change of costume if you can. That frock is truly *naff*.'

I looked down at it. It was my best dress, and Hal had chosen it.

'Who should I ask for if I want a change?'

'Production office has the lists. But there's no need to hurry. They're still setting up.'

The great thing about film sets, as I soon discovered, is that everyone assumes that you know where you're going so no one stops you. I found the production office, and by some miracle Arabella as well.

When she saw me she clapped a hand to her mouth to stifle a scream.

'What have they done to you?' she gasped. 'Oh my God, Lottie. Who or what on earth are you meant to be?'

'A guest at the big party scene,' I said, thickly, through a layer of bright red lipstick.

'What sort of a party giver would ask the likes of you?'

I felt tearful.

'He thought I should look like Vivien Leigh.'

'You look like Medusa. You just need a few snakes coming out of your hair.'

'He also said I should get a better frock. Can you arrange it?'

Arabella looked down the list.

'I think you'd better be a different kind of guest,' she decided. 'I'll put you down as *Scary Guest*. You might even get a line or two – but forget the new frock. The one you are wearing is quite terrifying enough.'

Arabella did not know it, but her arbitrary judgement of my Vivien Leigh look could not have been worse for me. The rest of the guests at the party were relatively anonymous, all being listed as *Party Guest #1*, etc., whereas because of Arabella's list, I had now been singled out. First of all, despite hiding behind a pillar, when I finally walked out I bumped straight into Melville, who gave a small shriek.

'What have they *done* to you, Heart?'

I tried to look nonchalant.

'*Scary Guest* in the party scene,' I said, tapping my chest indicatively.

'*Scary Guest* is about right. Just don't let Hal see you. He's the world's worst corpser.'

Even I knew that *corpsing* was theatre slang for laughing at the wrong moment.

But it proved impossible to hide from Hal as he came on to the set just when the Assistant Director was looking round for the party guests, finally calling: '*Scary Guest*, please? *Scary Guest*, come and stand here, if you would.'

I had been trying to hide behind a pillar but now had to emerge, feeling as if I was coming out on to the world's stage.

Not being used to filming, I had no idea that it was perfectly normal for everything to take an age while everyone frowned and moved cameras and lights before frowning some more and moving them all back again to where they were originally. When I was standing where the Assistant Director indicated *Scary Guest* should go,

Hal of course spotted me, although at first – as he told me later – only by recognising my dress.

Of course he started to laugh. He laughed so much he had to leave the set for a drink of water.

Melville remained calm throughout while giving me I-told-you-so looks before the director arrived surrounded by a flurry of attendants, all of whom looked incapable of decadence.

'What is this?' he asked his Assistant Director, staring directly at me.

I attempted to look innocuous, just any old extra standing about not wanting to do anything much except be helpful.

'This,' the Assistant Director told him, 'is someone called *Scary Guest*, Chief.'

I don't know why but I had expected Leslie Robertson – this famously up and coming film director – to be taller and somewhat fetching. In fact he was the very opposite: a small man wearing a collarless shirt and smoking an untipped Gauloise. He looked me up and down and frowned. He obviously didn't remember ordering up any *Scary Guest*.

He looked over at Hal, who was trying hard not to look at me.

'Silence, everyone!'

Silence except from the returned Hal, who once again started to laugh helplessly.

Ten minutes and several glasses of water later, Hal, his makeup repaired, was at last laughter-free, but only because I had been escorted to the back of the party scene. As I was dutifully milling about with the other extras a tall bespectacled young man looked at me with sudden interest, although not the kind that girls are usually meant to invite.

'I daresay you got the Gus treatment,' he said, nodding at my hideous hairstyle when there was a lull in proceedings.

I agreed that I must have.

'The dress is mine.'

He stared at it.

'I should leave that in costume and find something else,' he said in a kind voice.

'My mother's dressmaker made it for me.'

'Very kind of her, I am sure, but take my advice and leave it in costume and ask them for something a little bit more chic.' He leaned forward and whispered in my ear. 'And get rid of the slap. You're really very pretty, you know.'

Harry Bart was at RADA studying to be a proper actor. I found this out when we broke for lunch. I was impressed, but at pains not to show it.

'I thought that was just a place for debutantes to pass the time of day.'

'No – no, that's the other place, although we do have some,' he conceded, taking his glasses off. 'But mostly

181

we are ambitious young people striving to become stars, and have our own trailers, before taking on vast Shakespearean roles and getting knighted.'

I sighed. It all sounded so much more fun than being in MI5 and trying to defend the nation's security.

'What do you do when you're not being a party guest?'

'I work in … the War Office,' I said, quickly correcting my near treasonable error.

'The War Office? But not all the time, surely, or you wouldn't be here?'

'Oh, no, not all the time, but some of it. I'm a secretary. You know – shorthand and typing and that kind of thing.'

The moment I mentioned shorthand and typing, Harry looked interested.

'I can't type,' he said. 'Think you could teach me? I want to learn how in order to write scripts in which I can star.'

'Do you have a typewriter?'

Of course he didn't have a typewriter, but since we had one back in Dingley Dell, before I knew it I was offering Harry the opportunity to come and learn on it, while he was offering me the chance of a different chair in makeup, well away from Gus.

'Can I give you a lift home?' he offered.

'I have a lift, thank you.'

I suddenly realised it was not quite the thing for an extra to climb into a chauffeur-driven car with the film's leading actors, so quickly changed my mind.

'Actually I would prefer to go home with you. I felt a bit sick in the car I came in this morning.'

Harry dropped me off at Dingley Dell, before driving on to Earls Court where apparently he was sharing a flat with some Australian male models.

The next morning I still shared the car with Hal and Melville, who had at last stopped teasing me about my role as a scary guest.

'I see from the script, Lottie, that today you're a factory worker toiling away at your loom,' Hal boomed from the back of the car. 'Oh, dear, yesterday was bliss. I fully expected Comrade Robertson to explode when I went. I haven't had a corpse like it since playing Malvolio at Guildford Rep.'

After that, the talk in the back of the car between Hal and Melville was once more kept low although I did manage to catch different words, and phrases, the main one being *motivation*, as well as lavish praise for each other's performance.

'That's bad,' Harry told me later over lunch. 'Actors should never discuss each other's performance – it takes the edge off. Probably why it all went so badly this morning. How about Leslie? He was in despair.'

It was true the director's face had grown ever bleaker as Melville and Hal played the scenes exactly as they must have been rehearsing them in the car. The gist of his fury was that the actors were playing their parts all wrong.

Finally Leslie took to sermonising, during which monotonous and really very long political diatribe Melville stared at nothing at all. He just fiddled with his prop gold cufflinks leaving Hal to take the floor, which he very willingly did.

'My dear old Heart,' he finally boomed at Leslie, when the director had at last finished his sermon. 'Not all factory owners are bastards, and not all workers are saints. So why not shake off the clichés and let us play fully and properly rounded characters?'

There was a long silence followed by the crew suddenly bursting into applause. Hal of course looked round at them and bowed.

'There will be nothing for you or anyone else to play unless you do as directed,' Leslie quietly warned him in return. 'And if you're not very careful and don't all come to your senses, I shall close the picture down,' he told his rebellious cast and crew.

'So now who's being the horrid factory owner?' Melville murmured, with an audible sigh.

I had no idea why my father had been so interested in sabotaging Leslie Roberston's film, but seeing how intransigent Melville and Hal were being about the interpretation of their roles, I realised that he must be using the same tactics that communists were adopting to cause strikes in factories, he was getting at the target from the inside, and of course, actors being actors, Melville and Hal were thoroughly enjoying themselves. The car journeys in the morning were lightened by the sound of their laughter as they planned yet more fiendish antics destined to throw Leslie Robertson into chaos and confusion.

For myself, I was having a grand time on the factory floor. Gone was the Vivien Leigh makeup and in its place was a ground-down lady with a scarf tied in the accepted manner – knotted on top of my head – and a blacked-out tooth.

'I think you should lose the tooth over lunch,' Harry said, shuddering slightly. 'Or at least do me a favour and don't smile.'

'It's more fun than being *Scary Guest*, except I got myself pushed into my loom by Hal this morning.'

'You should toughen up,' Harry said, looking patronising.

For revenge I smiled at him.

'You make me feel sick when you do that,' he grumbled.

'Well, people in those days couldn't afford to go to a dentist, even if they could find one. They had to tie a tooth to a door knob, then get someone to slam the door.'

'My grandmother used to do that with us,' Harry said, lighting a cigarette. 'It always worked.'

I was impressed, but seeing that he seemed to have all his teeth, I didn't quite believe him.

'It's great if you have what we used to call a wobbler – you know?'

I changed the subject.

'What are you doing after the film?'

'Finish at RADA and starve, really. And you?'

'Back to being boring at the War Office.'

'Of course it's not the only thing you do.'

'No,' I agreed. 'It's not the only thing I do. I also teach out-of-work actors how to type.'

'Yes, you do, don't you?'

Harry smiled suddenly while quickly putting a hand on my mouth so I couldn't smile back.

'Is the quick brown fox going to be coming round to my flat this weekend?'

This was his way of asking me to pinch my parents' typewriter and bring it round to him, instead of smuggling him into the house and letting him have a go on the Olivetti when they were out at cocktail parties or away at weekends with friends with large draughty houses.

'No – you'd better come round to us as usual.'

The truth was I was worried that if I nicked it for even a few hours, I might be in very hot water. My father might need it suddenly and immediately, for doing stealthy things.

'Come round on Saturday morning and with luck it will be free. The ancestors don't get up until late on a Saturday as Mrs Graham doesn't come in until midday and they don't know how to boil an egg, so Saturdays they diet and sleep.'

Harry duly presented himself at the front door of Dingley Dell, only to be told to go down the area steps and knock on the dining-room window, which I would open for him.

'Do all your friends come in this way?'

'Some do, some don't,' I said, indicating the typewriter. 'Now don't look at the keyboard, just stare ahead and try to remember where everything is.'

I was feeling pretty nervous just for lending him the wretched thing – anyone who knew my father would know why – but Harry had a way with him, and I have to admit that it was not the kind of way I was used to. He made you want to adopt him; even though you knew that by helping him it would be sure to turn out the worse for you – you still went ahead and did it. It was actually quite annoying; nearly as annoying as watching him trying to memorise the keyboard, or tap out the wretched fox jumping over anyone and everyone.

I was in the kind of nervous state that comes over me when I think I am doing something wrong but am going ahead with it anyway, when the dining-room window was flung open and a policeman's helmeted head appeared. Harry jumped up, at the same time losing what little colour he had. As if that wasn't enough the dining-room door opened too, and my father appeared in his best Chinese silk dressing gown, blocking off any possible escape route.

'What are you doing, Lottie, may I ask?' he asked in his calmest voice, which is actually his most terrifying. As he had his swordstick in his hand, I felt I had to tell him the truth.

'I'm teaching Harry – this is Harry – to type on your typewriter,' I said, trying to sound normal.

My father glanced at the typewriter and Harry's forlorn effort.

'Not getting very far then, are you?'

'Is this all right with you, sir?'

The policeman stepped over the sill into the dining room, a large sheaf of papers in his hand.

'I suppose it has to be, Constable,' my father said, hanging his swordstick on the back of a dining chair.

'So nothing missing then?'

'Only normal good manners,' my father stated, staring from Harry to me and back again.

There was a sudden silence during which all four of us realised we were terribly embarrassed, the policeman not least. He cleared his throat.

'About these parking offences, sir.'

'Yes, of course.' My father nodded at him. 'Come upstairs and I will settle everything with you.' He turned to me. 'You may put back the typewriter and tell your friend here there is a very good night school on Kensington High Street, and the next time he climbs in anyone's dining-room window, do two things – close the window afterwards and don't do it in full view of a policeman.'

My dressing-gowned father departed with his usual measured gait, followed closely by the policeman who turned to me before he left and muttered, 'Sorry about this, Miss Lottie. Wouldn't have got you into trouble for all the world.'

After he had gone Harry stared at me.

'He knows you?'

I sighed. I had forgotten that PC Hobbs came round once a month on a Saturday morning to sort out my father's innumerable motoring offences, which must all come under the Official Secrets Act, because my mother had told me that since he had to be in such strange places at such strange times, normal motoring rules couldn't apply to him.

'It's difficult to explain,' I said, a little hopelessly.

'I only did what you told me to do,' Harry said, climbing back out of the dining-room window.

'No, wait,' I said.

He turned.

'Might as well finish the lesson.'

'But what about ...?'

Harry pointed at the ceiling and we both imagined PC Hobbs and my father together upstairs, muttering about streets and roads and traffic lights, and scribbling things.

'My father won't be down for hours. He has a bath on Saturday mornings where he washes his hair and sings his favourite songs. And PC Hobbs will leave by the front door.'

Absentmindedly, I picked my father's swordstick off the back of the dining chair and dropped it. It fell apart. Harry stared first at it and then at me.

'No point in asking, I suppose, is there?'

I slowly shook my head and just as slowly put the blasted thing together. No, there was no point in asking, but for a few seconds as Harry went on staring, which was only understandable, I was tempted to tell him that my father was a spy and life at Dingley Dell was always like this. But then I realised it would probably mean I would go to prison, and I didn't fancy that much, so I shut my trap and settled for wishing once again that my father was a stockbroker, or a merchant banker – any profession where he would not have to go about with swordsticks and other weapons.

That was the last morning when a fox jumped over a lazy dog at Dingley Dell. The Olivetti was returned to its normal place, and Harry joined the night school where I would meet him afterwards. We would go for a coffee and plan a glittering future for him, one where he starred in his own plays and became rich and famous. Neither of us ever referred to the swordstick or the policeman again. Perhaps we both sensed it was one of those episodes in life when the less said the better, but for many weeks he avoided coming within even spitting distance of Dingley Dell, and we both knew why – especially me.

INTERROGATIONS

Arabella was back in the Section working for Rosalie. I had expected her to be moving on to greater things, but it seemed she had turned down promotion on the understanding that work in the Section could be made more exciting for her. It was philanthropic, patriotic, and I was most impressed – until I realised that the promotion would have meant Arabella missing out on lunches at Fenwick's.

'Don't want to go to Brackenwood House,' she told me over a delicious Fenwick's salad. 'The atmosphere there is too concentrated.' She rolled her eyes. 'You know there's a rumour going around that the Section might be dispersed due to lack of activity?'

I had not known but now that I did I was put out.

'I'll speak to my father,' I said in my most show off-voice, which is actually very unattractive.

'Your father will think of something,' Arabella stated as a matter of fact. 'After all, it was thanks to him that I had such a great time in the *Why* production office.' She sighed, and I misinterpreted the sigh as one of regret. 'I have to say that after what I saw those producers get up to, I couldn't wait to get back to being with nice decent people like Rosalie, and spies. Oh, and you, of course,' she added, rather too late.

At Dingley Dell that evening I blocked my father's way to the drinks cupboard and asked him about the rumour going around that my Section was about to be disbanded due to the lack of genuine activity.

He gave me one of his looks, as always accompanied by a long silence.

'I'll think of something. New ideas needed. I'll find some,' he said, eventually.

I believed him because my father never made false promises. I stepped aside as his gaze had now switched over my shoulder to the drinks cupboard.

I was actually feeling vaguely indignant about the Section and the rumours about it, in a way that surprised me. I had not realised the affection that I felt for the place and all the good people who worked in it. I waited patiently for something to come of my father's promise to me, and sure enough a few days later I was called into Commander Steerforth's office.

He was feeling excited. I knew this because he had a pencil in his hand with which he was tapping out Morse code. When he was feeling excited – perhaps with chocolate cake in the offing – he liked to send the signals zipping across his desk, just like in the old days, to warn of a destroyer or a submarine. I knew this because he always warned me if I was in the way.

I waited for him to sink a destroyer or warn of a stealthy submarine before he told me what the exciting news might be.

'The Section's taking a new direction, it seems. Word has come in from Brackenwood House,' he said in an excited voice. 'We are to start on exercises as soon as possible, in the Section – not on Salisbury Plain or anything like that.'

'Nothing involving security films?' I asked nervously.

'No, no – this is to prepare ourselves in the event of another war.'

I tried to look nonchalant, which along with some of my other facial expressions was not a winner. I knew this because Commander Steerforth leaped to his feet and fetched me a glass of water.

'We are not prepared for all eventualities ... any eventuality really. What if there was an attack on the Section? We're just not prepared.'

He stood up and I don't know why I knew that he could hear the sound of the sea, and that he felt he was alone on the bridge again, swaying along with the movement of the rolling waters below. I suppose it helped that he kept flapping his hands and muttering, '*Dratted seagulls.*'

'I daresay we will have to practise things like inter-rogation? In the event of war we might have no MI5 officers – or even, say, nurses or doctors?' I suggested.

When I saw Commander Steerforth's expression light up, I wished I hadn't mentioned interrogation.

'Yes, yes,' he said thoughtfully. 'Interrogation tech-niques will certainly have to be gone through.' He went to his desk. 'I have a handbook here somewhere.' He took out a pristine volume. 'Yes, here it is.' He opened it, and then put it down. 'Best go through it later. It looks a bit technical'.

I quickly flicked through it when he left the room.

Chapter One was entitled 'Shoes'.

Just my sort of book, I thought, only to be sadly disil-lusioned when I discovered the opening paragraph was entirely lacking in any reference to fashion.

'*The first rule is always to make sure that you remove the suspect's shoes because it makes it more difficult for him to escape.*'

I put the book down. It felt like cheating to read it before anyone else had, even Commander Steerforth.

He came back into the room

'Jolly good idea about nurses,' he said enthusiastically, 'we could get you all uniforms from some theatrical agency or other, couldn't we? And perhaps a matron's outfit for Miss Lovington?'

'Oh, no, actually it is not a good idea,' I said, quickly. 'We can miss out on that, really we can. There's a first-aid box under the stairs with Miss Lovington's old ashtrays. It's never been opened so all the bandages and plasters must be quite unused.'

'Even so some nursing practice would be useful, I should have thought. We can borrow stretchers from somewhere, or a front door – used those in the war – and really get something practical going. Let's make some notes, straight away.'

I picked up my shorthand notebook and pencil, ready for further ideas.

'Now on to interrogation exercises. I wonder how we should go about this ... military fashion, of course. Close the Section, take one or two people – say a couple of the ladies from Files – and ...' Here he consulted the pristine booklet on his desk. 'And remove their shoes. That way they will not run away. Although,' he read on a little further, 'it would be good if they tried, and we brought them down with a rugger tackle *then* took their shoes off.' He paused, looking thoughtful. 'We never took shoes off in the Navy, you know.'

'What did you do?'

'We threw them overboard.'

'After interrogation?' I asked, suddenly more interested.

'Oh, no, before. Then we threw them a rope, and hauled them back on board, and held them upside down to get the water out of them.' He sighed, nostalgically. 'Mind you, I actually don't remember getting anything useful out of prisoners after that. They were always too wrecked to remember their own names, let alone naval manoeuvres.'

I was looking at Commander Steerforth with renewed respect. He had experienced proper warfare. I knew I must concentrate better on interrogation exercises.

'So,' I said, pencil poised, 'I suppose we'd better work out the first interrogation exercise. Is it up to us to start?'

It seemed it was, and there was no time to be wasted. He started to dictate a plan based loosely on what he had already outlined. Naturally we both agreed that our plan must rely on secrecy, no one else must know it and we must not know anyone else's, so whatever Arabella and Rosalie might be planning was up to them, because, as Commander Steerforth pointed out, Chapter Two of the handbook stated 'Surprise is Essential'.

I chose Doreen in Files because I knew she had finished her jumper and had a bit of time on her hands until her new wool arrived. Commander Steerforth was happy with this. He liked Doreen because she was always so cheerful, he said, but how best to surprise her?

He thought the better way would be to send her out on a mission to the canteen, and surprise her there. This we duly did.

'Doreen,' I said after our sudden arrival. 'We are arresting you on suspicion of being a double agent.'

She looked at me with one eyebrow raised.

'Lottie dear – we all know this is an exercise.'

'No, Doreen,' I said, happy that there was no one else in the canteen. 'No, this is real life, and there is a war on.'

Commander Steerforth was guarding the door. I stepped forward but so did Doreen, and with one very effective movement threw me sideways.

'Oh, dear,' I said, picking up the canteen chair that had interrupted my fall.

'Sorry, Lottie,' she said as she helped me up. 'I used to throw sides of beef to the lions in my father's circus, before I took up knitting.'

I straightened up.

'Well, do you think you could remove your shoes anyway?'

She gave me an old-fashioned look.

'Oh, very well, but only once I get into Commander Steerforth's office. I don't want to get a splinter.'

Once in the office she removed her shoes and sat down in my chair opposite Commander Steerforth, who had his handbook out and was slowly turning the pages.

'Now, Prisoner Number blank, blank – I want you to tell us what you were doing lurking about in the canteen?'

'You sent me for some Victoria sponge, Commander Steerforth, remember? About five minutes ago.'

'Oh, yes, so I did. And then what happened?'

'Lottie here tried to arrest me and I threw her into a chair.'

I was hovering at the back of the room, but at this I stepped forward.

'May I take over here for a minute, Commander, because I know the prisoner quite well?'

Commander Steerforth nodded.

'If you want,' he said a little hopelessly, and quickly turned the pages in the handbook to try and find further help before surrendering his place to me.

'Doreen,' I said in a kindly voice, 'you must know more than you think after being in Files for so long. A great deal more has seeped into your brain than other people realise, wouldn't you say?'

I thought I was giving a good imitation of my father, staring unblinkingly at her. I think it must have been better than my other looks because Doreen stared back at me, looking a bit put out. At any rate she agreed she did probably know more about the files than she or anyone else gave her credit for. Before long, by giving an imitation of my father's technique when he found me back late from a party, I had her admitting to a know-ledge of the contents of the PFs and even the SFs that not even she had realised she had.

'That was really very good,' Commander Steerforth said, after Doreen had put her shoes back on and left the room, saying she was happy to have been of help. 'Your father does that, you say? All that staring and looking away? Most effective.'

He turned the pages of his booklet, and I saw that he was now skipping to Chapter Three – 'Interrogation'.

I left him reading and went to thank Doreen.

'What did you think? I mean of the way we handled you … if you had been, say, a communist aggressor?'

Doreen looked at me, and her expression was far too kindly to make me feel confident of her reply.

'We had more success in the circus getting the lions to sit on the drums,' she said, before nodding towards Arabella, who had emerged from Rosalie's office looking startled.

'She's not having too good a time with Pauline,' Arabella said, with some satisfaction.

'Well, she wouldn't. Pauline was an ARP warden in the war,' Doreen informed her.

That evening I approached my father in some concern. I did not want to give the Section away, but I needed to know more about interrogation. What had been his methods in the war, for instance?

'Easy,' he said. 'Give them a bottle of whisky and a kindly smile, tell them how sorry you felt for them, and they were so grateful you weren't getting out the thumbscrews they would tell you anything. Glass of wine?'

I readily accepted the wine while mentally making a note that I had better tell Commander Steerforth and Rosalie about this, because judging by the suppressed laughter we heard every time we passed Files, we were not doing very well.

Back with Arabella in the Section, I was not in the least discouraged by the fact that we had used the wrong techniques. I told her what my father had done to get information out of spies and double agents during the war.

'We can't give them whisky,' she said, with some justification. 'Most of Files are teetotal.'

So my father's wartime technique was ruled out, and instead we turned our thoughts to other things – namely Commander Steerforth, who was now looking very depressed, so depressed that not even a slice of Victoria sponge would cheer him up.

I instinctively knew that his depression was so serious I would have to go about tackling it very carefully, thoughtfully, and avoiding all possible hurt. Commander Steerforth was a widower of some years' standing, which meant that the Section was virtually his second home. Of an evening he went back to a lonely poached egg on toast, or spinach – he did vary it with ketchup, he told me – and the wireless. His weekends were spent walking in the Park and talking to people with dogs, because his landlord did not allow him to have one of his own. He liked fishing but that could only happen when he was on leave, so his life, as far as I could tell, was a bit limited. This was why I had to be so careful. One word out of place and he might spiral ever downwards.

'Sometimes,' I said dramatically, putting down my pencil very suddenly when we were in the middle of a piece of particularly boring dictation, 'you can feel got down by something and that no one can help you at all – that you are in the middle of nowhere, no flowers are growing, and there are no trees blossoming.'

He looked immediately concerned.

'Is that how you are feeling?'

'Yes,' I lied.

'This is not like you at all, Lottie, you're usually the life and soul of the Section – posters on the filing cabinets and all that sort of thing. Shall we ever forget that lovely one of Marilyn Monroe? Then bright suggestions of all kinds – and you're a wonder at producing cakes, even bringing them from home. No, Lottie, you must not be got down, no, no, not you.' He stood up. 'Tell you what: to cheer you up, I will get you cake instead of you getting me some. You know, officers and men in the regiment? Once a year the officers wait on the men. It cheers them up no end – the men, I mean, not the officers.'

'No, no – no, really, no cake, please.'

'I insist.'

Minutes later, looking triumphant, Commander Steerforth came back from the canteen with a cake on a plate. I stared at the cake and then at him and my heart sank. It was a bun stuffed with coconut, which has always made me feel sick – not the bun part, the coconut – but looking up at his happy expression, I knew that this bun had to be eaten, no matter what. While he thrust the plate at me I thought of the things people do for England and, really, eating coconut was very little compared to the war, and bombs, and things like that.

'You really enjoyed that, didn't you?' he said when I had finished chewing.

I nodded and, making my excuses, quickly made for the Ladies'. It would be indiscreet to say any more, but when I emerged Arabella accosted me before I could return to take more dictation.

She always called Commander Steerforth *the blood-hound* on account of his expression and his jowly cheeks.

'I know why the poor old bloodhound is down in the mouth,' she confided. 'Last night Rosalie interrogated him, in her office, without his shoes and everything, and guess what?'

I shook my head. I couldn't guess anything.

'He told all.'

I stared.

'All what?'

'You know – all – everything to do with his work in the Section.'

'How did she manage to get it out of him?'

'Simple, she gave him a couple of whiskies and was nice to him. Apparently it was what—'

'They did in the war,' I said, finishing for her. 'I told you that.'

I thought what with my undoubted courage as regards the coconut and the excitement of the interrogation of Files that the Commander would cheer up after that, but he didn't. So I confided in Arabella then, telling her how worried I was about my boss. Work was becoming really sad, with the Commander never smiling, just permanently morose, and no Morse code on the desk or being plagued by seagulls.

'He has let himself down. Men don't like that – Monty told me the other day. He says women couldn't give a damn, but men mind dreadfully. And for the Commander letting himself down in front of a woman is even worse than it would be with another man.'

'How is Monty?' I asked, to change the subject, and even as I spoke I thought I could smell his cooking, and see him making the perfect breakfast.

'He is perfection,' Arabella said with some satisfaction. 'Utter perfection. It's my mother who is the problem. In spite of everything she is missing Sergei, would you believe? Monty is a great success but Sergei loved the arts, and especially the theatre, and she misses that so much. Monty does his best to please her – but Sergei and she had a sort of understanding.'

I thought I knew what that must be, but I kept my trap shut as MI5 trains you to do. For all I knew it was

Chapter Four in the Commander's handbook – 'Keeping the Trap Shut'.

'Why don't we get Commander Steerforth to come round to dinner with Mater?' she suggested.

'Do you think that would work?' I asked, not daring to tell her that I knew about Mater and her role as a double agent, and so did the Commander.

'Oh, yes, I am sure it would. Anyway, if it doesn't, at least he will get a good dinner.'

We neither of us knew how to go about it. One wrong word from us and both our victims would stall – that much at least was apparent.

Monty came up with a plan, which Arabella relayed to me the next day.

'Nothing to do with Trigata?' I asked, fearfully.

'Oh, no – no, we have quite dealt with that, I think, although as Monty says, you can never quite be sure with import–export businesses. Never know what new fumes will be circling in the air above as they smoke their fish.'

'Never,' I agreed, remembering Trigata's heavy foreign accents on the telephone.

There was still so much to be thinking about, what with Harry going up for a part at the Shakespeare Memorial Theatre, and Hal giving him coaching which was driving Mrs Graham mad because, given that they were rehearsing in the dining room, they distracted her from her cooking in the kitchen next-door. As I say, so much was happening at Dingley Dell that for a few days I forgot about Mater and the Commander.

Melville was shooting a film in the Highlands and Islands, which meant that his room had come free for a few days, and that must have encouraged my father to say that his aunt Bibby could come to stay.

Fresh from the African jungle where she had fled with the love of her life, she was now a widow and eager to catch up with the rest of the family.

'Oh, Lord – here she is,' my father murmured, and put his drink down.

We both stared at Aunt Bibby, being followed by a taxi driver who was carrying the kind of suitcases that must have seen many torrential rains, and been more used to being carried through the jungle on the heads of tall young men with perfect balance.

'Dear boy,' she said, kissing my father effusively, to which he submitted with surprising grace.

'This is Lottie.'

'So it is. Good! Wanted to meet my only great-niece for as long as I can remember.'

Aunt Bibby only stayed a few days, just long enough to give me a whiff of what it was like to live in the jungle and never see another white face except that of your husband.

'Bliss, dear, utter bliss,' she told me when I took her a cup of early-morning tea, and sat on her bed to chat. 'It is the only way for man and woman to live, believe me, the only way. Just the two of you ... and the animals, of course, plenty of animals. You remember that, always.'

Of course I thought I would, but when I told Arabella she merely rolled her eyes and said I couldn't live without other people – that I just wasn't the sort.

By the time Aunt Bibby left Dingley Dell to move on to seeing new sets of relatives, her marvellously old-fashioned clothes trailing behind her, large hat insecurely balanced on a precarious mound of once chestnut hair, Arabella and I had finalised our plan to bring Commander Steerforth and Mater together.

I had dropped a hint that I thought it would be a good idea for him to see Mater, in case, in the following months, the Section was closed and scattered to the four ends of Brackenwood House.

'She is, after all, Arabella's mother, and it could do you nothing but good if you are moved on to another Section. You will know that she is a firm contact for you,' I said, sounding a little too maternal even to my own ears. 'Arabella has told me that her mother would be delighted to meet you, and asked if you might like to go round for dinner on Friday night?'

Commander Steerforth looked thrilled, and then suddenly shy.

'I haven't had dinner alone with a lady for a very long time,' he confessed.

'Oh, you won't be alone, Arabella and I will be there …'

He looked disappointed.

'… for drinks,' I added hastily. 'And Monty will be there to serve dinner. You'll like Monty. He's a wonderful cook.'

'It will make a change from poached eggs,' Commander Steerforth joked. 'Informal? Just black tie?'

'Something like that,' I agreed,

'Tails are not worn now, are they? Not for dinner, not since the war.' He sighed nostalgically. 'And even then, you know, they were going out of style.'

Arabella thought she had arranged everything quite superbly, and indeed she had, until Commander Steerforth arrived and Monty opened the door to him.

The moment they clapped eyes on each other the flat was filled with joy.

'Miss Arabella never told me our guest was Commander Steerforth! I served under him in the war, and a better man could not be found.' Monty adjusted his wig excitedly. 'Of all the Commanders for Madam to have to dinner, it had to be Commander Steerforth … my Commander. Life can surely get no better.'

He bustled back to the kitchen, leaving us to take the guest in to drinks.

I wish I could say that the moment Commander Steerforth saw the Mater it was love at first sight but of course it wasn't. It was, however, quite cordial enough to make Arabella and I feel happy to leave them together for dinner while we went off to the cinema and supper on our own at Dingley Dell.

'Do you think it is safe for you to go back now?' I asked, eventually.

'I'll make loud throat-clearing noises before I go in,' Arabella joked.

I went to bed that night, thinking more about Aunt Bibby and her exciting stories of eloping to Africa than I did about Mater and Commander Steerforth, so when I arrived back in the Section to find Arabella looking both calm and excited, which only Arabella could, it was almost a foregone conclusion that Mater and the Commander had got on like a house on fire, especially since I knew he thought so highly of her wartime career as an SOE agent.

'It went like clockwork,' Arabella reported in the canteen over coffee and a bun, thankfully without coconut.

'So you are the fairy godmother, and our dear Commander will be as cheerful as a cricket on a hearth?'

'Oh, no, nothing to do with me,' Arabella stated, putting her special spoon back in her handbag. 'No, no, all to do with Monty. He cooked up a storm apparently – all the Commander's favourites – although how he knew, *searchez-moi.*'

'Not difficult. The Commander eats anything,' I said, tersely. 'Even his own cooking.'

'At any rate, it is all arranged. He is to take Mater to a play next week, and before long I am sure they will marry late in life and Monty will be their bridesmaid.'

'What did they have for dinner?' I asked, suddenly feeling suspicious of Arabella's reticence on that subject.

'You don't want to know.'

'Yes, I do.'

'Lobster.' Arabella assumed her sphinx-like expression. 'Let's just hope it was from Harrods and not Trigata, Lottie.'

FRIENDS, ROMANS, AND COPPERS

Life back in Dingley Dell was as always full of incident, what with spies coming and going all the time. We
seemed to be taking care of a great many spy demands:
everything from taking calls from their agents, to entertaining their dogs or girlfriends. My mother was the soul
of patience, but her martyred expression spoke of inner
turmoil, and she made up for it by going to Stratford to
see a great many productions, most of which she found
to be less than good, but at least it gave rise to some
good discussions with Melville.

My father also came and went all the time, but never
once asked how life was in my Section. I started to
suspect that the new plans for us had not been a success
with the top people. I knew Commander Steerforth
and Rosalie had done an excellent job of making the
interrogations seem expert, and authentic, and we
had all endured First Aid practice to the satisfaction
of the Red Cross although thankfully without donning

costumes. Commander Steerforth's security booklet had now been read through, not just by him but also by me. I have to say that the advice about what to do in the event of an atomic bomb dropping on the Section was, to my mind, a little light on solid fact. I could not see why getting under a table might help, nor pulling the curtains, particularly since in our Section we didn't have any.

I said as much to the Commander but he was now too busy dreaming about taking Mater to the theatre to pay much attention. Arabella was also distracted, busy making plans to travel to Greece when her leave came up, which was probably why she was so busy practising her French. Harry was away working on a film where he had one line, a line he was quite excited about. It was '*How nice of you to meet the train, Mrs Davenport*', which together we had rehearsed umpteen times until even I knew how to say it. So when our neighbour – an artist – asked me to sit to him, for want of something else to do at the time, I readily agreed.

I say 'readily', but the truth was that no sooner had I agreed than I regretted it. I was certainly not going to tell my father because Van was an old friend of his from their days together at Oxford, and I had the definite feeling that he would not approve.

I knew where Van's studio was, and it was comfortingly near to Dingley Dell. As I headed there I told myself that, perhaps more importantly, it was on the ground floor and so easy to get out of.

I had already planned my escape before he opened the door.

Van stared at me. He was a tall, well-built man with a great shock of blond hair and startling blue eyes. He wore the kind of clothes that faded so well you knew they had once been very expensive.

'How many cardigans are you wearing?' he asked curiously.

'Two,' I said as sunshine flooded the studio room. 'I'm a rather cold sort of person.'

'Even so, perhaps you would like to remove one?'

I shook my head, thinking that if I did it might be a slippery slope, and the next thing he would want would be for me to remove another, until I was sitting to him in my vest.

I sat down on the chaise-longue he had provided, and looked around me with some interest. I'd always liked painters' studios, and had the feeling that most people did because they had an air of adventure about them, as if the room itself knew that anything could happen there, at any time. A masterpiece might be born or a sudden revelation lead to a new artistic movement – or, judging from some of the drawings on the wall, models of both sexes might start twisting their bodies into some pretty funny poses.

'So you're too cold to remove any of your woollen clothing?' asked Van, lighting a Gauloise and staring at me as if I had nothing on at all.

I nodded, and then thought quickly.

'Good title for a famous painting, though, don't you think?'

'What?' he asked, a little edgily, as he continued to stare at me seated on the chaise-longue.

'"Girl With Two Cardigans" by Joachim Van Cleft,' I suggested. 'It would be the talk of the Summer Exhibition.'

He thought for a minute.

'Yes,' he said, 'and you're right – a good title for a painting makes for a good sale. I like that.'

I was beginning to feel a trifle hot, but I would not, could not, let him see that in case he wanted me to strip down to my vest. Besides he had started sketching.

As he did he stared at me. Saturday morning was not always the best time to be at Dingley Dell as poor Harry had discovered, but now I felt as if Van, as he was always known, had X-ray eyes, and while he stared at me I was required to hold the rather boring pose he had put me in on his chaise-longue. I started to long for a normal Saturday morning, when I would go to Portobello Road and see a friend or two, and we would wander about pretending we knew all about the antiques that were on sale.

'Don't move!' Van kept saying that. 'Don't fidget!' While he himself was dashing backwards and forwards, either to his ashtray or his coffee pot. Or his telephone, which rang constantly.

I wouldn't have minded if he'd had long interesting conversations, but it was always the same sort of chat, no matter who was ringing him. From the tone of the conversation this end Van seemed to be very much in demand, and his dialogue was along the lines that Harry would call *now drag me ons*, whereby he ended up allowing himself to be taken out by some yearning female. With Van it was always: '*Oh, very well, if you think I will enjoy it.*' Or: '*Well, if you think you can afford it, darling.*' Listening to him, I realised that older women were much bolder than I'd thought. I also had the feeling that Van was someone who expected women to come after him, which was what Arabella always called *interesting.*

At least the telephone calls gave me time to wiggle my feet or scratch my nose before he turned round and started booming at me not to fidget.

It didn't take long for me to start feeling sorry for all those models made to lie in cold bathwater with their long hair freshly brushed, while some over-zealous Pre-Raphaelite puffed and panted at his easel. But unlike me they'd had no other choice because most of them were very, very poor and very, very beautiful, and if you are very, very poor and very, very beautiful everyone knows you always pay for it. It is just one of those given facts, like millionaires always being tight with money and putting slot machines on the toilet doors, or telephone kiosks in the hall.

These thoughts were occupying my mind when the telephone rang yet again at the same time as there was a knock at the front door. Van went immediately to answer it because he was expecting a new supply of paints and canvases from somewhere up North. I was glad that he had to check through everything because it meant I could get up, and stretch, and it also gave me an excuse to pick up the telephone and pretend to be someone else, which is always a good way to pass a boring few minutes when nothing is happening except time passing by.

''Allo?' I said, doing what I thought was a good imitation of Arabella speaking bad French. 'Nathalie speaking. Can I 'elp you?'

I had it in mind, if it was one of Van's many older ladies, to pretend to be a model so as to make them jealous. I have no idea why but I had always thought French models the world over were called Nathalie, and the very idea that they might be called anything else had never occurred to me.

But the voice at the other end was all too familiar. And if I am going to be honest, it was one that, had I not been wearing two cardigans and a vest, I would have said made my blood run cold.

By the time Van came back into the room I had resumed my pose, because I didn't want him to know what I had done. More than that, I suddenly did not want to arouse suspicion.

'Who was that on the telephone, Lottie?' he asked.

If he had known me better Van would have known I was lying because when I lie I always open my eyes too wide, but as it was he didn't know me at all so when I said, with eyes as large as coffee saucers, that it was a wrong number, he seemed to accept it readily.

From then on, I suppose like all guilty people, I lived the whole morning in dread of another call from the same source. I could not wait to *scarper*, as Harry called it, or *hightail it out* of there. And hightail I did, slap on the dot of one o'clock, with the best excuse in the world, namely that Mrs Graham was making my favourite lunch.

'You're a somewhat greedy person, aren't you?' Van grumbled.

I agreed I was before leaving without paying any attention to the painting, or the sketch or whatever it was that I had been sitting to him for.

'I do hope it's not a portrait,' my mother sighed when I confessed how I had spent the morning. 'You wouldn't want anything that looks like you, Lottie. And no nudity, or silliness like that. Van is a bit of a ladies' man, you know. Not that he would be interested in you, I don't suppose.'

After a delicious lunch in the garden, I approached my father hoping that he might be in a good enough mood to hear what I had to say without getting crusty.

'What it is, you see,' I began, distracting him from the rest of the people there.

He gave me one of his looks.

''Allo, 'allo,' he said in a very bad cockney accent, which he sometimes did after a few drinks of a Saturday. 'What 'ave we here a-then?'

'It's probably nothing really,' I began as his frown deepened, probably because he saw my mother had put the cork back in the wine bottle. 'The thing about it is, I went to sit to Van this morning—'

'Dog sit, did you say?'

'No, you know, sit to him. As in for a painter.'

My father frowned.

'Why on earth would you want to do that?'

'Well,' I said, feeling as if I was drowning, 'I don't know really.'

'Seemed like a good idea at the time?'

I was rather touched that my father was obviously trying to be helpful.

'Something like that,' I agreed. 'As I say, I don't know why I did, but I wore two cardigans and a vest.'

'Wore a suit of armour, eh?'

He tried to keep a straight face, and for a second I saw that side of my father that everyone else seemed to and I rarely did.

'Yes, that kind of thing,' I agreed. 'At any rate,' I continued, speeding up because I could see he was about to be bored, 'his phone goes all the time, and it's always women.'

'Same old Van, eh? I think women like men with thick hair, you know.'

'And then when he was out of the room, for a joke, I picked up the telephone and pretended to be a model called Nathalie.'

'Why would you want to do that ?' my father asked, frowning. He was very correct and I could see that picking up someone else's telephone was a bit of a breach of etiquette, but pretending to be someone called Nathalie might be the last straw. Never mind that he spent his whole life doing things like that. It was in the service of his country, whereas this was just me horsing around.

'I was a bit bored from sitting on the chaise-longue. At any rate, that is not why I want to tell you about all this.'

'Well, that's a relief anyway.'

'No, what's important was who was on the other end.' My father was still bored. 'You see – you see, the caller was Trigata.'

Suddenly he wasn't bored at all.

'You're quite sure?' he asked, dropping his voice to spy level. 'I mean absolutely sure?'

'Absolutely quite sure,' I said. 'Utterly so, in fact.' I had answered the phone to them so many times at Mater's flat that I would know them anywhere. The same thick foreign accent. The same urgency, the same demands about their dreadful fish.

Once again to my amazement, I saw that my father could move very quickly when the need arose. Before I could say another thing he was in his car and gone.

'He hasn't had his second pudding,' Mrs Graham grumbled. 'That's not like him at all. He always has two at the weekends – like clockwork he is with his favourite puddings.'

I knew not to tell anyone or a contact might get blown, so I lived with this Trigata knowledge all week, coming in and out of Dingley Dell and never seeing my father because he was obviously on the track of something. Finally on the Sunday evening of the following week, after his usual sing-song with Melville and a riotous lunch with other guests, or spies, for all I knew, he called me into his study. Going into his study was not something I liked doing, but on the other hand if your father works for MI5 and he wants to speak to you there's not much you can do about it.

'Jolly good, Lottie,' he said. 'You did well.'

I glowed. I couldn't help it. I couldn't remember him saying anything like that before and so I felt rather proud of myself.

'I've had a bit of a ponder, and since you're in this far I suppose there's no harm in letting you in a little more. We have a lead, you see – several leads in and out of a labyrinth of people in high places. And lower down too. I'm afraid my old friend Van might be on the list. But I can't be sure. So we're going to have to go back to basics and try and draw these people out, Van included. A poultice is what is needed, to draw out the poison – if there is any.'

I was impressed. I'd never heard my father use words like *poultice* before.

'I've given this some thought,' he continued, 'and I think the first thing to do is throw a party.'

'A party?' I gasped. 'What – to celebrate that there's a leak?'

'No, no – nothing of the kind,' he replied. 'Simply to open a door of opportunity.'

I was still getting over the shock of my father suggesting giving yet another party, because it was so surreal. He invited the whole world into his house, he gave them drinks and food, but parties were simply anathema to him. It was all so out of character.

'We often need access to where certain people dwell, you see,' he explained, sounding a little Shakespearean.

'Need a bit of room to roam. So I thought perhaps a party. People never say no to a party, apparently.'

Except you, I wanted to remind him, but it was about to get even worse.

'I thought a nice fancy dress party, with a title. Not Vicars and Tarts for a change. Something a little different.'

'Such as?' I wondered, clearing my throat.

'I thought Romans and Greeks perhaps – although, please God, not too many blasted Greeks.'

I knew that my father had a thing about Romans, and no time for the Greeks whom he considered a bit on the flouncy side, but the idea that he would ask everyone not just to turn up to a party, but to dress up fancy for it, was almost beyond belief.

'We're going to get cracking at once – this needs to be activated immediately. We'll invite certain people on the list, including our painter friend, and while they're all disporting themselves as Greeks and Romans – he will be a Greek, I would have thought – our people will go and take a quiet shufti at his place. If we can find a way to draw the poultice we will save a lot of lives, and that is what our job is all about. Making things safe.'

'That's what Commander Steerforth says,' I agreed. 'That MI5 is all about preventing bad things from happening.'

'Yes,' my father agreed. 'And you have just played your part. Now all we have to do is hope for a bit of a lucky break.'

I spent the rest of the week walking so tall that Arabella grew suspicious.

'Are you and Harry still going out?'

'Sort of. Why?'

Arabella looked sphinx-like.

'Nothing.'

'He's working on a film out in deepest Hertfordshire. He's got another one-liner. It's: "*Quick! We got to get out of here! The cops are at the door!*"'

'Sounds like more than one line to me,' Arabella replied, thoughtfully, typing the words out in the air.

'By the way,' I asked, to divert attention from Harry, because I never like to admit my feelings about much, and Harry was drifting out of the pals and friendship zone into something more grown-up, 'are you coming to my parents' party?'

'Of course I am coming,' Arabella returned. 'The whole Section is. Rosalie says she's going to come as a Grecian urn.'

I had thought I'd get out of going back to sit to Van, but my father reckoned that might be a bit suspicious. He thought it better for me to return and act innocent.

If there is anything I am rotten at it is acting innocent. The moment I have to act innocent and guiltless, I become suffused with guilt and feel as if I'm covered in those arrows prisoners used to have all over their uniforms.

'You can always wear three cardigans,' my father joked.

Happily the weather had turned cold so that my inner sweat did not turn into outer sweat as I yet again posed on the wretched chaise-longue, and Van smoked his way through a packet of untipped Gauloises and several telephone calls whose content I prefer to forget. I tried not to look at my watch, because I knew that would make him even scratchier than he was already but the three hours seemed to crawl by, and what with the rain pouring down and the telephone calls, it was more of the same but worse somehow.

Happily, or unhappily, depending on how you look at what happened as a result of all this, he ran out of cigarettes and decided to dash out to the corner shop for more, leaving me in charge.

I have to tell you I willed the telephone to ring and for it to be Trigata. I looked at the clock. It was just about the same time as last Saturday, so I willed it and willed it, and finally the phone did ring.

'Trigata?' I asked before they could speak.

'Yes,' said the thick foreign accent. 'You take call for recipient of import?'

'Yes,' I said. 'I take call.' I was not bothering to be Nathalie. 'And the same order is wanted by the recipient importer but this time to go to—'

Again one of those moments came over me, moments where I seem to lose all normal control and two horns pop out of the top of my head. 'Yes, same order, different address.'

I heard myself giving the address of Dingley Dell; not only that, but I actually had the audacity to ask them for lobster.

The owner of the thick foreign accent exploded.

'*No lobster!*' he screamed in a thick foreign way, which made the sound more like a thirty-second warning. '*I tell you, no lobster!*'

I put the receiver down and thought for a minute. My first notion was that Arabella might be right and lobsters were some particularly high-security number – some sort of gun, or something – or perhaps a bomb of some kind. My second thought was that Mrs Graham might be able to do something quite nice with the fish, if it ever arrived, because she was good with fish. My last thought was to scarper, which I did, leaving a note for Van to say I would be back next Saturday, that my mother had phoned and I'd had to go to her at once as she was having trouble with her feet.

Actually she was having trouble with more than her feet. She was having trouble with the Roman and Greek party that my father was insisting upon. She was going as a Greek and my father was going as a Roman, and this was causing something of a rift between them.

'Your father has no respect for the Ancient Greeks. He thinks they should be sent back their marbles, or whatever we filched from them, and be done with it, and he will not countenance the idea that I should be hostess wearing a Grecian gown, but I insist on my own choice of dress. I met Van in the street yesterday and he is going Greek, and Melville is going Greek, and Hal is going Roman, if he can make it, which I don't think he can.' She looked mournful. 'Even Melville is less than happy, coming on after the performance – but you know how it is. Your father won't believe this but actors hate fancy dress – Melville told me. No, they don't just hate it, they loathe it, because that is what they do all the time. It's only what actors call civilians – people like me and you – who like dressing up. And it *is* expensive. I mean, the yards of material it is taking to make my gown will mean bread and gruel for the next few weeks.'

My mother going all Dickensian and referring to bread and gruel was not a good sign. It meant she was very cross but not showing it. I knew the signs, because she did not like Charles Dickens and least of all his novels, seeing him as a man who exaggerated the toils and moils of the poor, and portrayed women as nothing more than ineffectual drips. She once told me she thought it was sheer cheek Oliver Twist asking for more. She maintained that he should have thought of the other children before himself and waited his turn.

I felt guilty when I left her, as indeed I should have done. If I had not become embroiled with Trigata, and then Van, she would not have had to shell out for a Grecian gown, and Mrs Graham would not be threatened with an influx of fish.

There is something about an event you are dreading with all your heart and soul that makes it hurtle through the normal processes of time, if not the eternal verities. If the said event is going to be a cracker, it takes forever to happen, but if you sense there is going to be trouble and yet could not quite say what shape it might take, if you in other words absolutely dread the day arriving, it seems to come about in seconds, not even minutes.

'I hear there is going to be an orgy between Romans and Greeks,' Hal boomed down the telephone at me. 'I shall make it whatever happens, if only to set my peepers on your blessed father dressed, Melville tells me, as a Roman. I shall join him, but then it's simple for me. I just have to woo the wardrobe mistress and get her to lend me Olivier's old toga.'

The Grahams too were going as Romans, which gave my father great pleasure.

'I am lending Mr Graham some of my upper-arm bracelets,' he told me, in the confidential tone he only ever used with waiters when asking about soup. 'I haven't told him that only Senators were allowed to wear them – don't want to hurt his feelings. He is also going to wear one of those hairbands, which I think will suit him.' My father breathed out with some satisfaction, before lighting a cigarette. 'I think if we are going to win this one, Lottie, we will win it by this party. I really think this might be just the ticket.'

There are certain expressions that offspring learn to note and my mother moaning about bread and gruel was a sure sign of dissatisfaction, whereas if my father mentioned something being just the ticket, I always knew he was feeling benign, at ease with the world, or, in this case, just about to trap his most hated of adversaries – namely a traitor.

I still had to sit to Van, of course, and I have to admit to feeling bad about it, which was probably why I went as always wearing two cardigans. I had told my father about the fish from Trigata being redirected to Dingley Dell, and found to my surprise that he thought it a good idea.

'I say, Lottie,' he said, 'you really are intent on earning your corn.'

Which made me feel very tall, which I am not.

As it transpired Van was in a mighty good mood, looking forward to the party that evening and showing me his Grecian costume with great pride.

I stared at it, arranged in readiness on the bed. Would he be arrested in it? I knew policemen took away things like shoes and belts. I tried not to think of poor Van without his Grecian sandals, and his Grecian robe sagging for lack of its piece of stranded silk, which passed for a belt. I hoped and prayed that he was innocent, and that Trigata was going to turn out to be a mistake. All these feelings must have made me a poor model, because he sent me home early.

The house was what Arabella, who was staying with us, called in her newly acquired French *en fête*. White cloths covered the tables in the dining room, and flowered garlands attached to the cloths did give them a Romanesque look. Mrs Graham had been prompted to try out a few Roman dishes, a very rich chicken pie among others, but drew the line at Grecian.

'I told your father I don't mind doing some of these Roman-type recipes he gave me, but I've steered clear of the Greeks. Stuffed vine leaves your mother asked for, and I have done those – but some of the other dishes I will not attempt. Tomatoes, tomatoes, tomatoes! Didn't they use anything else in Ancient Greece? And as for this salt cod and heaven only knows what else that arrived this morning, I will not touch the stuff.'

Mr Graham was on the door as usual, taking cloaks and toga covers, but looking less than usual himself. The upper-arm bracelets my father had provided for him were just the job but his circlet made of twists of metal kept slipping so Arabella wound it round with some of her velvet hair ribbon and it clamped down better.

Actually, far from being a dreaded event, the party began and went on to really swing. Everyone had made an effort, and of course the candlelight and the flowers gave it a properly festive look. It also meant that Arabella and I had a job keeping an eye on Van, who had arrived looking marvellous, his great head of blond hair styled *à la Grecque*, as Arabella put it – there was no stopping her French now.

Dinner was being served late to accommodate so many of the actors, who came on from the West End, or in Hal's case, very, very late indeed, but Melville was not in the last act of his play, so he was able to break the rules and miss his curtain call, which was a theatrical crime, but, as he said, 'forgivable just the once'. He was playing one of my father's favourite numbers when there was a crashing knock at the front door.

'Not more fish,' Mrs Graham sighed as I followed Mr Graham upstairs, all too aware that it was one of those evenings where I was needed everywhere.

Of course Mrs Graham had ignored me about the delivery earlier, and had unwrapped it and put it in the fridge, and after a cursory look I knew there were no guns or anything anywhere so stopped worrying – although something Mrs G said she'd found in the bottom of the box and duly handed to me certainly gave me – as they say – some pause for thought dot-dot-dot.

I fled upstairs because I knew I had to keep an eye on Van whom Arabella was busy distracting, making sure that he imagined she was available as a future model.

I had hardly edged into the drawing room to announce that dinner was being served when there was renewed heavy knocking at the front door. I saw Mr Graham going to open it with his now statutory greeting: '*Citizens of Rome and Greece — welcome!*' — then, on seeing who was on the doorstep, I immediately stepped back into the drawing-room doorway. It was only the police.

'We're here to see the owner,' I heard one of them say somewhat grimly. 'Kindly inform him of our presence.'

Mr Graham then adjusted his Roman circlet and gave them his best hard stare.

'Sorry, gentlemen,' he said. 'It's Romans and Greeks only as per invitation. You can't come in dressed as policemen. Orders is orders, so I'm afraid if you want to come in, you'll have to go home and change. And if you do, please note it's sandals only on account of the rushes on the floors. We do not want them trodden in. Thank you.'

He closed the door on them and came back into the drawing room where I saw him taking my father aside and obviously informing him of the arrival of gatecrashers. My father gave him one very quick look, then taking hold of the most recently arrived guest, whom I'd never met, hurried the poor chap quickly out of the drawing room and downstairs at top speed – whereupon the knocking resumed at the front door only more so.

Once again discreetly following Mr Graham back into the hall, I watched as he drew himself to his full height and opened the door to confront the gatecrashers once more.

'You do not seem to have understood what I just said,' Mr Graham began with studied politesse. 'No plods, just Romans and Greeks.'

'And you do not understand what I just said,' the officer replied, showing him his warrant card. 'We are the genuine article and we are here to speak to the owner. *If* you do not mind.'

Intending to go and find my father and warn him, I spotted Policeman Number Three, who only turned out to be the one known as my father's parking policeman.

'Miss Lottie?' he called to me. 'It's purely routine, Miss Lottie. We just need to speak to your dad.'

'Not more parking tickets?' I said in what I hoped was a genuinely sympathetic tone. 'Can't they wait?'

But by then the police had gained entry, only to find themselves confronted by my father who, far from appearing disconcerted, appeared to be in rather a benign frame of mind, judging from his smile – an unusual sight at the best of times.

'If you're here to arrest me, Inspector,' he announced, 'I have to point out that as a Senator of the Roman

Republic, I can only be arrested by a person of similar rank and standing.'

'We are not here to arrest you, sir.'

'Senator, if you don't mind.'

'We're not here to arrest you, I assure you. Not unless we find due cause. We're here, Senator — I mean, sir — because there's been a break-in locally and the resident who witnessed it says he later saw the possible perpetrator of the crime fleeing the said house and running in this direction. After giving chase, he says he then saw the possible perpetrator entering this very house. I wonder if you could be any help in this matter, sir? Senator.'

'*Nullus nullus verbatim hic*, alas, old chap. Sorry,' my father replied cheerfully. 'All our guests are invited and accounted for — excluding your own good selves. Do come in and make sure, though. I think my wife and my daughter here can back me up.'

Not mentioning, of course, the person unknown whom my father had whipped post haste out of the action only moments ago, unobserved by anyone except me.

After allowing the police access to the party, my father then despatched Mr Graham back to his duties but remained by the front door with me until everyone else was out of earshot.

'It's fine, Lottie,' he murmured as we stood facing the closed front door. 'Our bird is safely flown. But he has left us a little egg.'

Between thumb and forefinger my father held up a very small roll of film.

'Something found in the suspect's paint box,' he said quietly. 'Roll of microfilm. Might be quite interesting to see the photos, I would say.'

'Yes,' I replied, feeling a sudden welter of relief that perhaps it had all finally in a way paid off – although if this was the case, I felt really sorry for my father because he and Van had known each other since University.

'Oh, but there's something else,' I added, hurrying after my father before he made it back into the party. 'Mrs Graham found this at the bottom of the box of fish.' I handed over her findings – a plastic-covered file that contained some sheets of typed paper. 'At first glance I thought they were just invoices – but if you take a look, you'll see they appear to be written in some sort of code.'

'Well, I never,' my father said, almost to himself. 'Lottie. Whatever next?'

'As long as it's all right,' I said. 'For a moment I thought I might have bodged it.'

'Not in the slightest,' he replied. 'Not even in the slightest.'

The Senator of Rome then padded off into the party, to return a moment later with his friend Van held firmly by one arm, followed by the police.

'No need to make a fuss,' my father informed them, obviously to save his old friend's face. 'But I think this is the chap we want. All of us.'

Nonetheless I still couldn't help feeling guilty about my own part in the downfall of a possible spy and said as much to Arabella the next day over breakfast.

'At least if it's true they won't shoot him, because it's not wartime,' she replied. 'And let's face it – it made the party even more exciting. Your father bravely pretending that arresting Van was just a hoax in revenge for a prank Van had played on him once. That was – that was–'

'Just the ticket?' I offered.

Arabella smiled, sphinx-like.

'Yes,' she agreed. 'Something like that.'

I felt relieved, but I think mostly because she hadn't said it in French.

P. S.

I knew I had to wait until Arabella had finished her prawn salad before she produced the buff-coloured file from her handbag. She looked round before handing it over to me. I opened the file to reveal the book I had recently just finished writing on the second-hand type-writer recently gifted to me by my father.

'Of course,' she began to say while producing her personal spoon, which for some reason I found vaguely menacing, 'you do know this will have to be destroyed? Such sensitive material cannot be left in people's hand-bags, especially not mine as I have signed the Official Secrets Act and will not go to prison for you.'

'That wasn't why I wrote it.'

I promptly borrowed her spoon to stir my coffee, which always annoyed her.

'I wrote it because I wanted to get it down some-where. It's more like a diary really.'

'Of course, you know no one will believe it?'

'Of course.'

We laughed, because suddenly we both found it hilarious to think that other people might read it and definitely not believe a word.

'I hope Harry hasn't read it,' she said.

'No, no, Harry wouldn't read it – he only reads scripts, and then only the bits that he is in, which sometimes makes for quite a quick read, you bet.'

'Which bit do you think they will definitely find unbelievable?'

I thought for a moment.

'Laetitia dropping the security films down the lift shaft. Definitely a bridge too far in the believability zone.'

'Really? I think Trigata is the bit they'll have trouble believing.'

'Yup. They'll find that too fishy, won't they?'

'How about the actors and the film? That might be a bit of a push for them.'

'Oh, yes,' I agreed. 'And Hal being set up as a political figure, all that trouble ending with a wartime buffet.'

Arabella tapped the file in front of us, suddenly looking nervous.

'This is highly dangerous material. It will have to be destroyed,' she insisted. 'Unless …'

She resumed her usual sphinx-like expression.

'Unless we think of something else, which we should be able to do.'

I knew I had to come up with something.

'You mean like burying it in a garden somewhere for future generations to dig up and find?'

'That's about right,' Arabella agreed. 'You haven't told your father about it, of course?'

'Gracious, no, he would have a twin fit. He would think,' I tapped the file, 'of this as letting down the Service. Have me put up against a wall and shot. For bringing the Service into ridicule and disrepute, and so on.'

The thought of him reading the contents of the file really rather silenced us.

'So,' Arabella continued, 'there is only one copy, and I take it it's anonymous.'

'Unless the authorities track down the owner of the Olivetti with the two worn Ss.'

'You see,' Arabella continued as if I hadn't spoken, which was a habit of hers, 'my point is this. You have made a record of the way things really were, and let's face it, it would be a pity if it were all lost forever. I mean, Rosalie and the Commander, the ladies knitting in Files, all the different adventures we had … they are a sort of tribute to the good-heartedness of what my old granny used to call "folk". Good folk and true, working away in the defence of our lovely country, full of integrity, and so much fun, really. Because we have had fun, haven't we?'

I nodded. I had never known Arabella like this. She was almost sentimental.

'So what do you think we should do with it.'

I too tapped the file. Now we were discussing things so deeply it seemed more like a ticking bomb between buff-coloured covers.

'I think,' Arabella announced, 'that we should put it in an SF and hide it at the back of Rosalie's files.'

'Why Rosalie's?'

'Because she was in SOE during the war and no one will ever dare touch anyone in SOE. Too jolly brave, etc. We will hide it there under a mountain of her older files, and when the old files get taken away, which they always do, and stored at Kew under wraps for fifty years, there will be your account of MI5 in the fifties. QED. Fool-proof ... completely fool-proof. The chaps at Kew can never be bothered to look through all the files. They just hurl them into the right spots, and rush off for a cup of tea. I know because Rosalie told me. It rather annoys her, actually. She says they must have buried a great deal that could have been useful, but there's nothing to be done about it.'

'I think you may have had what Harry calls a super wheeze.'

'I think I may have too,' Arabella agreed, her expression at its most solemn.

'So you hide my book inside Rosalie's old SF files, knowing that no one will go through them? Off to Kew they go, only to be opened up to public scrutiny in fifty years' time?'

I looked past Arabella with a dreamy expression as I imagined, in the distant future, solemn-faced people wearing little white gloves, all staring wide-eyed at my account of life in MI5 in the nineteen fifties.

'Supposing they trace it back to us?'

'Who cares?' Arabella replied, shrugging. 'But one thing it has proved, Lottie, is that Olivetti did not live in vain.'

'Oh,' I said, surprised. 'Thank you.'

'Actually – I don't know about you – but wouldn't you give anything to see the look on the faces of those white-gloved military historians? They really won't believe a word.'

'Yet you know, and I know, everything in the book happens to be true.'

'Which is why no one will believe it.'

I sighed, pretty deeply, because of course I knew Arabella was right.

END

P.P.S.: Let's face it, you didn't – did you? Not a dicky bird of it. So take off the little white gloves and go home.

In Memoriam Terence Brady 1939–2016

Wherever he was there was joy and laughter

ABOUT THE AUTHOR

Charlotte Bingham wrote her first book, *Coronet Among the Weeds*, a memoir of her life as a debutante, at the age of 19. It was published in 1963 and became an instant bestseller. She went on to write a further memoir, *Coronet Among the Grass*. Her father, John Bingham, the 7th Baron Clanmorris, was a member of MI5, where Charlotte worked as a secretary. He was an inspiration for John le Carré's character George Smiley.

Charlotte Bingham went on to write thirty-three internationally bestselling novels and, in partnership with her late husband Terence Brady, a number of successful plays, films and TV series including *Upstairs Downstairs* and *Take Three Girls*. She lives in Somerset.

charlottebingham.com

ABOUT THE TYPE

The text of this book is set in Perpetua. This typeface is an adaptation of a style of letter that had been popularised for monumental work in stone by Eric Gill. Large scale drawings by Gill were given to Charles Malin, a Parisian punch-cutter, and his hand-cut punches were the basis for the font issued by Monotype. First used in a private translation called 'The Passion of Perpetua and Felicity', the italic was originally called Felicity.